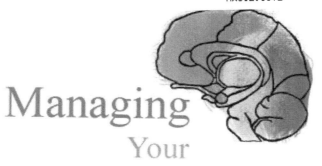

Managing
Your

BRAIN

Managing
Your

LIFE

By Jerry Mungadze, PhD

Copyright © 2016 by Jerry Mungadze, PhD

Managing Your Brain
Managing Your Life

ISBN-13: **978-1983532443**

Published by Sound Mind Publications
A division of Sound Mind Programs
1901 Bedford Drive, Suite 608
Bedford, TX 76021
www.soundmindprograms.com

Printed in the United States of America

All Scripture quotations, unless otherwise noted, are from the *New International Version (NIV) of the Holy Bible.*

CONTENTS

INTRODUCTION   4

OVERVIEW OF THE BRAIN   6

MANAGING YOUR THINKING   19

MANAGING YOUR PERCEPTIONS   27

MANAGING YOUR EMOTIONS   34

MANAGING YOUR REACTIONS   43

MANAGING YOUR IDENTITY   50

MANAGING YOUR BEHAVIOR   59

MANAGING YOUR RELATIONSHIPS   65

MANAGING YOUR SPIRITUAL LIFE   75

MANAGING YOUR SPIRITUAL BATTLES   87

EPILOGUE   98

Introduction

During my doctoral studies at the University of North Texas, I developed an interest in brain physiology: the parts of the brain and their specific functions. This interest intensified when I began treating people who had experienced severe psychological and spiritual trauma, and I quickly realized that typical approaches to therapy weren't very effective, especially with trauma victims. As a result, I have conducted extensive research on the brain and its functions and on trauma and its effects on the brain.

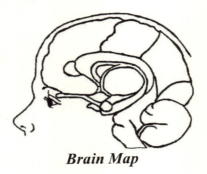

Brain Map

Throughout my years of practice, I found that people who suffered from trauma commonly turned to nonverbal and symbolic language—including drawing, music, and arts and crafts—when they were unable to find the words to express themselves. I encouraged my clients to use pictures and colors to represent their feelings, thoughts, beliefs, and behaviors to help us better understand the problems they were experiencing. When doing so, they often were not consciously aware of the information they were conveying. But because these right-brain modes of expression represented a safer way of articulating suppressed traumatic experiences, their brains were actually using them to reveal things that were buried in their subconscious minds. This discovery, along with my greater understanding of the workings of the brain, led me to develop Right Brain Therapy (RBT).

RBT offers a way to see, hear, understand, and resolve the effects of trauma using therapeutic approaches that bypass the left brain and open the door to the real person inside: the person most freely expressed by the right brain. This freedom of expression is the key to mental and emotional healing. And the most effective tool for expression is what we in RBT call a brain map: a simple unlabeled drawing of the parts of the human brain. When I asked my clients to place pictures and colors into the various divisions of a brain map, a whole new world of understanding was unlocked.

From their completed brain maps, my RBT-trained associates and I can tell how our clients perceive themselves and the world around them, their beliefs, their fears, and their predominant feelings. We can see how well they control themselves and their impulses and whether they have any addictions. We can determine if they have faith and if they are under any forms of spiritual attack. Their brain maps reveal whether they've been traumatized and, if so, what types of trauma they've experienced.

All of this is possible because our brains record and project this information. You see, God designed our brains to perfectly run every aspect of our lives. As David expressed in Psalm 139:14, our brains are fearfully and wonderfully made!

It's hard to argue with the success of the RBT model. Over the years, countless numbers of people have experienced the power of RBT to accurately express their internal worlds. By learning how the areas of their brains work and affect the ways they function, perceive, feel, behave, react, relate, and dream; they have been able, with God's help, to drastically improve the quality of their lives physically, emotionally, mentally, and spiritually. And you can too!

Before you start your journey, I want to be sure you understand an important point I just made. You can drastically improve the quality of your life *with God's help.* This treatment approach combines the science of RBT with the power of Scriptures and the guidance of the Holy Spirit. So together, let's begin.

Chapter 1

Overview of the Brain

For you created my inmost being;
You knit me together in my mother's womb.
I praise you because I am fearfully and wonderfully made;
Your works are wonderful,
I know that full well.
My frame was not hidden from you
When I was made in the secret place,
When I was woven together in the depths of the earth. Your
eyes saw my unformed body...

Psalm 139:13-16

In 1989, I conducted a study that verified a consistency to the meanings of colors in the color spectrum to my therapy clients. At the time of this discovery, many therapists were assigning collages to help their patients express themselves, and some of my clients began bringing collages to their sessions. Though they all chose their own content, I began recognizing a pattern to where each of them chose to put that content on the page. As a further experiment, I asked my clients to make color and word collages to go along with their picture collages. They were free to place their pictures, colors, and words anywhere they liked across the page. I soon learned that it didn't matter what type of content my clients used; their three different collages communicated exactly the same messages every time. The meanings of the colors matched the meanings of the pictures which matched the words put in the specific locations.

It was then suggested to me that I offer each of my clients a drawing of the brain to color. Taking into account the functions of the various parts of the brain, I was curious to see if the colors they chose to put in each area would communicate any messages about their lives. Amazingly, even though I had not provided my clients with any information on the functions of the parts of the brain, the colors they chose to put in each section communicated the same messages as their collages did. The more I observed my patients and the way they colored their brain drawings, or brain maps, the more I realized how much can be learned about what's happening to a person by reading what he or she expresses through colors, pictures, and even words put in the different sections of a brain map.

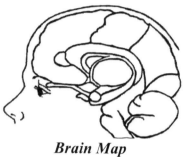

Brain Map

When a new client arrives at our RBT clinic for counseling, he or she is first given a brain map to color. No instructions are provided as to how it should be colored, and the client is free to make his or her own choices. The miracle of brain mapping is that it helps my associates and me pinpoint our clients' problems and their root causes so that we are able to help direct their brains towards healthier ways of functioning.

Though you must be an RBT-trained therapist to truly understand how brain maps provide important information, you will find a working knowledge of the different areas of the brain and their functions to be a tremendous tool in your quest to manage your brain and, thus, manage your life. To that end, I would like to take you on a tour of the brain and show you the ways each section impacts the different areas of our lives.

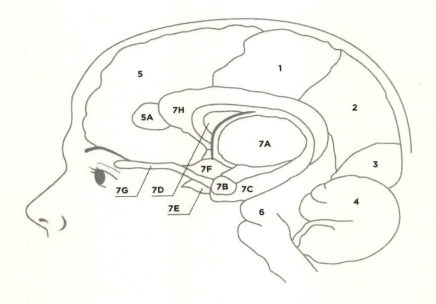

1   **Motor and Sensory Cortex of the Parietal Lobe**
2   **Perception Part of the Parietal Lobe**
3   **Occipital Lobe**
4   **Cerebellum**
5   **Frontal Lobe (Includes 5A)**
5A **Broca's Area**
6   **Brainstem**
7   **Temporal Lobe (Includes 7A-7H)**
7A **Thalamus**
7B **Amygdala**
7C **Hippocampus**
7D **Basal Ganglia**
7E **Pituitary Gland**
7F **Hypothalamus**
7G **Olfactory Bulb**
7H **Corpus Callosum**

The Motor and Sensory Cortex of the
Parietal Lobe (1)

The motor and sensory cortex receives information from the outside world and influences how we perceive the world and those around us. It also determines how we function in our relationships. Many poor relationships are caused by issues such as hyper-defensiveness, hyper-alertness, fearfulness, aggression, anger, clinginess, neediness, over-sensitivity, or over-emotionalism that are revealed in this part of the brain.

Clearly, relating well is crucial to the human experience; we all relate to one another in some fashion. So, how healthy are your relational patterns? Poor relational patterns don't just impact your relationships. They can affect your identity and ability to function.

We all know people whose relational patterns are very unhealthy. For example, many people in the world today seem to thrive on work and take pride in how busy they are, but despite their busyness, they are actually very lonely. We also know people who are good at the mechanics of their jobs but lacking in their interpersonal abilities. For instance, a pastor's poor relational skills may cause him to be overly sensitive and unable to receive constructive criticism from his elders. He may be adept at preaching sermons, but his problems relating well to people hinder his ministry. At our clinic, my associates and I know to focus on the motor and sensory cortex when we see these types of unhealthy relational patterns.

The Perception Part of the Parietal Lobe (2)

The perception part of the parietal lobe influences who we believe we are and contains our dreams, fantasies, and wishes. Our wishes and fantasies (which commonly show what we are lacking) along with any problems we may have dealing with reality reside in the upper section of this area of the brain. Self-perception resides in the lower section of this part of the brain, and this is the area from which we project all sorts of perceived identities such as, "I am a peaceful, contented person," "I am a go-getter," "I am strong and competent," "I am a loser," "I am what my family made me," "I am evil," etc. How we perceive ourselves profoundly influences our self-esteem, our daily functionality, and our interactions with others.

In Galatians 2:20, the Apostle Paul speaks of his former identity being replaced with a new identity in Christ. Many Christians say their identity is in Christ, and for most of them that identity is a positive reality. But this is not the case for all Christians. By using RBT, it is easy to identify someone who is truly experiencing his or her identity in Christ. In addition, since this is the part of the brain that is capable of spiritual perception, it is here that we can see both spiritual giftedness and spiritual struggles.

The Occipital Lobe (3)

The occipital lobe, where the visual cortex is located, is the visual center of the brain, but it doesn't just process the images our eyes capture. It is also the center of our internal vision influencing our hopes, dreams, and overall outlook on life. A strong vision and hope for the future, a positive outlook and belief for success, determination and drive to fight to the end, and motivation to beat the odds and overcome obstacles reside in this area of the brain. Characteristically, I have found that motivational speakers exhibit strength in their occipital lobes.

Experience has shown me that a person may have very troubled areas in the rest of the brain, but if the occipital lobe exhibits strength, he or she will function well. On the flip side, hopelessness and negativity in this part of the brain will produce an overall outlook that is bleak and pessimistic.

The Cerebellum (4)

Latin for "little brain," the cerebellum plays a very important role in the integration of attention, learning, sensory perception, and motor control. Located at the base of the brain, the cerebellum is continually getting updates and feedback from other parts of the brain and the body. For instance, it receives input from the visual cortex in the occipital lobe to fine-tune posture, equilibrium, and motor learning.

The genius in this part of the brain amazes me! Anything that brings detriment to our wellbeing—anxiety, depression, suicidal or homicidal thoughts, painful traumatic memories, or spiritual oppression—is restrained in the cerebellum in order to preserve functioning and safety for the rest of the brain. But since the cerebellum is designed to hold things that are harmful to us, when helpful things such as joy, faith, strength and protective impulses are contained there instead, it is often an indication that a type of sabotage is occurring.

Normally, my associates and I look at the cerebellum to see what serious issues people may have. If we find the same problems elsewhere in their brains, we know to focus on those issues.

The Frontal Lobe (5)

The frontal lobe—which includes the prefrontal cortex, the frontal cortex, and the Broca's area—is the "here and now" of the brain. It is predominantly where consciousness resides and what we use to function in our everyday lives. Here is where we have our self-awareness, behavior control, verbal expression, and organizational skills, and our ability to function takes a nosedive when problems crowd this area of the brain.

There are serious concerns when emotions overtake the frontal lobe. Hopelessness, anger, neediness, anxiety, over-sensitivity, and any other feelings that may result in "acting out" behaviors can take away functioning very quickly.

I have found that psychological trauma in the frontal lobe will produce an array of problems including attention deficit disorder (ADD) and attention deficit hyperactivity disorder (ADHD). These disorders disrupt the ability of this area of the brain to pay attention and stay focused.

The enemy loves to attack this region to cause us real trouble. Therefore, one of our first goals in RBT is to bring normalcy back to the frontal lobe.

The Broca's Area (5A)

Located in the frontal lobe, the Broca's area is known to control reactions in speech and movement to extreme fear or shock. But I have discovered that this region of the brain does so much more. My case studies indicate that the Broca's area is really command central for the front brain. It seems to influence, and can even override, all that is happening in the rest of the frontal lobe. This means the Broca's area is ultimately in control of our everyday functioning. It also appears to be involved in mastery and containment of our brain's most threatening issues which it pushes back into the cerebellum (4).

I have seen situations when all was well in the rest of the frontal brain but problems in the Broca's area—like anger and other emotions, control issues, or trauma memories—brought dysfunction to the whole frontal lobe. Consequently, when helping people heal from problems related to functioning at our clinic, we focus on the Broca's area along with the frontal cortex.

The Brainstem (6)

The brainstem is located at the bottom of the brain and includes the medulla oblongata and the midbrain. This area is the life support system of the entire body and is associated with the major organs critical in sustaining physical life. The heart, lungs, kidneys, and liver are regulated here, and injuries in this area of the brain can be fatal.

I have found that the brainstem can absorb emotional trauma from elsewhere in the brain. When trauma memories and certain psychological problems fail to be properly processed, those issues may leak into this area of the brain and inadvertently get stored as body memories. This can lead to an array of physical problems. In RBT, when we help people remember and psychologically process their traumas, these types of body issues are usually relieved.

The body and the emotional self are not as separated as people in the Western world seem to think. You may have heard people say, "I carry all my stress in my stomach," or "I carry my problems in my shoulders." These people are acknowledging the link between the emotions and the body. Many of the physical ailments people have are the result of unprocessed emotional issues. If we truly understood this concept, we wouldn't approach our bodies and our emotions as separate entities. I believe people who seek physical healing should consider emotional or inner healing first and see if their physical issues improve as well. We put too much emphasis on the body alone. We should emphasize the spirit first, then the mind, and then the body.

The Temporal Lobe (7)

The temporal lobe contains the limbic system which is a combination of several parts (7A–7H) that all work together as a unit. This area of the brain is the center of the human psyche. As the brain's own communication hub, it processes all incoming information from the outside world and from the body itself. The temporal lobe conducts the cognitive sorting of our experiences, stores those experiences as memories, and develops those memories into belief systems. Critical functions such as the regulation of hormones and appetites affecting eating, drinking, sex, pain, and sleep are in the temporal lobe. Fear responses are also handled here.

The Thalamus (7A)

The thalamus receives all sensory input entering the brain through the five senses and later disseminates this information to other parts of the brain for more processing. In addition, I have found—as have other researchers—that traumatic memories may be stored in the thalamus as sensory pieces of images, sounds, smells, tastes, and physical sensations but without the facts that tell a story. These sensory pieces can cause emotional distress, but they stay hidden from conscious awareness until they leak into the amygdala (7B) and the hypothalamus (7F).

I believe the thalamus, specifically, is the part of the temporal lobe where the human psyche resides. As the spiritual center of a human being, I believe it is the "heart" referenced in the Bible. It's here we find the things that are hidden in our hearts, and it's also where we find out deepest hurts.

The Amygdala (7B)

The amygdala is responsible for the fight or flight response. It serves as the brain's alarm system by sending signals to the front part of the brain when something is very wrong or threatening and triggering hormonal and other chemical responses needed in times of stress and danger.

When flooded with traumatic memories and sensations, as often happens with post-traumatic stress disorder, the amygdala causes all kinds of problems. My research indicates that the amygdala is the main cause of most post-traumatic stress overreactions. For example, when a veteran fails to recognize the war is over and continues to react as if he is still in the middle of combat, my associates and I know to look for trouble in the amygdala.

It's difficult to reason with someone whose amygdala is in an overactive state. A person must have a sense of safety in this area of the brain to be able to calm down.

The Hippocampus (7C)

The hippocampus sorts out all incoming information before it can be used in the conscious mind. It then presents a map for the rest of the brain to follow as it sorts and processes information. In addition, our experiences are stored as memories in the hippocampus which is equipped with the ability to retrieve them when needed. From our memories, the hippocampus builds the belief systems that influence our decisions and behaviors.

When it comes to traumatic memories, however, they seem to be stored in the thalamus (7A) as sensory fragments that do not make conscious sense. These fragments are behind the upsetting flashes experienced by those wounded by trauma. Whether they are distressing mental pictures, sounds, smells, or physical sensations, they need to be put together into an understandable story. As the reasoning aspect of our experiences, the hippocampus is responsible for this process.

There are many problems that occur when the hippocampus has itself been affected by trauma. One of the most common problems is the disruption of memory function. Some victims of trauma exhibit memory loss too vast to be explained by mere forgetfulness. Trauma survivors may also experience an inaccurate sense of reality. They form distorted beliefs that color how they interpret new incoming information. The following story illustrates how cognitive distortions can ruin communication and potentially good relationships.

The Psychotic Woman and the Twice-baked Potato

A young woman in search of a prospective husband held a dinner party at her apartment for a group of singles to enjoy as they mingled and got to know one another. Her hope was that a certain good-looking young man in whom she was interested would show up for dinner.

As guests began to fill the tiny apartment kitchen, this special man walked in and headed to the counter with all the food. Right in front of him was a plate of delicious twice-baked potatoes, but he chose not to take one, and the woman's heart sank in disappointment. She had hoped he would eat one of her potatoes, love it, and, ask who made it. That would launch them into a conversation that would lead to a date.

After a few moments, the woman approached the man and asked him why he hadn't taken a potato. He said, "I don't eat potatoes." Taking this statement personally, she asked, "So, you won't even try one of my potatoes?" He replied, "No, I'm sorry. I just don't care for potatoes." Feeling distressed, she responded, "Is it the way I prepared it that you don't like?" A bit surprised by her intensity, he answered, "I'm sure the way you prepared it is fine. I just don't like potatoes, no matter how they're made." To this the woman snapped, "Fine! I spent hours on those potatoes. And you won't even try one!"

Hoping complete honesty would calm the woman down, the man finally told her, "I'm allergic to potatoes. If I eat them, my throat swells and closes shut. I would have to be rushed to the emergency room." "So now you're accusing me of wanting to kill you!" she cried. Thinking, "This woman is psychotic," the man hurriedly left the apartment.

For the most part, our beliefs drive our behaviors. If we believe stealing is wrong, we are unlikely to steal. If we believe flying is dangerous, we will be reluctant to fly. But what happens if our beliefs are false? For example, what if a woman believes that most men can't be trusted? If she hopes to get married and start a family someday, it will be difficult for her to do so because of her false belief.

The Basal Ganglia (7D)

The basal ganglia are a cluster of neurons in the temporal lobe that functions as the brain's communication center. Messages coming from the basal ganglia, whether positive or negative, impact every area of the brain. If this section of the brain is inundated with things like anxiety or impacted by spiritual bondage, those problems will spread to the whole brain rather than affecting limited areas.

The Pituitary Gland (7E)

The pituitary gland produces hormones that affect our moods, appetites, and responses to physical and psychological threats. These chemicals are powerful forces that can influence our impulses and behaviors. We are all familiar with the issues that can result for both males and females when their hormones are out of whack. Females may experience premenstrual syndrome (PMS) with the resultant symptoms of anger, mood swings, depression, etc. Males may struggle with aggression, sexual impulse control, and issues with physical strength.

We cannot ignore hormonal and chemical reactions in our brains. Disruption of normal functions in this area can lead to serious problems ranging from a nonexistent sex life to criminal behavior.

The Hypothalamus (7F)

The hypothalamus is the regulatory area of the brain. It stimulates and inhibits the production of hormones and chemicals—particularly in the pituitary gland—and controls their interactions with various processes in the brain. I have found that discrepancies in these interactions are connected to addictive behaviours. When poor regulation of appetites by the hypothalamus affects hormone production in the pituitary gland, this can stimulate compulsive behaviours and lead to addictions.

It appears the prefrontal cortex, which covers the anterior part of the frontal lobe, follows directions from this area of the brain as well. The prefrontal cortex (which is not fully developed until age 24) is responsible for our impulse control, and I have seen variances in the hypothalamus affecting impulse management.

Traumatic memories may impact the hypothalamus. When sensory fragments from past painful experiences that are stored in the thalamus leak into the hypothalamus, intense emotional reactions may be triggered.

The Olfactory Bulb (7G)

Most of the literature I've read on the olfactory bulb says it's connected to our sense of smell; however, my own research suggests it is also involved in sight and other responses. One of the most important functions of the olfactory bulb is its ability to block the triggering of traumatic memories and sensations from the amygdala (7B). This is a major function given the potency of emotions and sensations that may be experienced when buried trauma is triggered by outside stimuli. The olfactory bulb tries to stabilize reactions in the amygdala and hypothalamus (7F). But when the olfactory bulb is itself filled with emotion or trauma, it only makes things worse.

People who suffer from addiction seem to have trouble in the amygdala, the hypothalamus, and the olfactory bulb. These are the areas where most anxieties, fears, depression, and other mood problems tend to take hold. Largely, what we refer to as chemical imbalance has to do with these structures in the brain, and it's important to know that willpower won't change the chemical reactions here. Thus it is necessary for some people to be put on medications for the problems they have.

The Corpus Callosum (7H)

The corpus callosum is the structure that manages feeling and rational states. With 250 million nerve fibers at its disposal, it integrates the emotional brain (the right brain) with the rational brain (the left brain). The corpus callosum is also attached to the Broca's area (5A) which initiates our speech and movement.

I sometimes refer to this area of the brain as "the feeling brain." The corpus callosum seems to translate all the functions in the rest of the temporal lobe into an overall feeling state that impacts the motor and sensory cortex (1), the perception part of the parietal lobe (2), the frontal lobe (5), and the brain stem (6). At our clinic, we have had patients who had areas of the temporal lobe that were filled with over-emotional, negative, anxious, and destructive states, but the trouble wasn't affecting the motor and sensory cortex or the frontal lobe as would normally be expected. This was because the corpus callosum was keeping everything in balance.

It is amazing to know all that happens in our brains! It's easy to see that they are not the result of some evolutionary, non-intelligent process but were perfectly designed by an intelligent, loving, redeeming God. But we live in a fallen world, and our brains were impacted by The Fall. Thus, though our brains do many wonderful things, problems can develop in them as well. When that happens, we need to take those problems to our brains' designer because He knows how they're supposed to work. God wants to redeem our brains, heal them, and bring them in line with His original design. That is the only way human beings can overcome adversity and reach their full potential.

Chapter 2

Managing Your Thinking

For as he thinketh in his heart, so is he…

Proverbs 23:7[1]

Finally, brothers and sisters, whatever is true, whatever is noble, whatever is right, whatever is pure, whatever is lovely, whatever is admirable—if anything is excellent or praiseworthy—think about such things.

Philippians 4:8

In the previous chapter, I highlighted the different areas of the brain and briefly explained their various functions. From this point on, I will present in detail the ways specific problems correspond to each area of the brain and provide exercises to help you effectively manage your brain to improve your quality of life. Let's begin with managing your thinking.

The way we think affects our feelings and behaviors. If we can learn to manage our thoughts, so many things in our lives will change for the better. As King Solomon said in Proverbs 23:7, man is what he "thinketh in his heart."

To manage our thinking, we need to look to the frontal cortex, the Broca's area, and the hippocampus. When scientists talk about mental decline, particularly in aging people, they are primarily focusing on functions of these areas. Because mental decline in the frontal cortex and hippocampus corresponds to a decline in productivity, this is a serious issue in every society. Thus, my goal in this chapter is to help you find ways to maximize the positive things these areas of the brain do for you and rid them of the things that negatively affect them.

---

[1] From the King James Version (KJV) of the Holy Bible

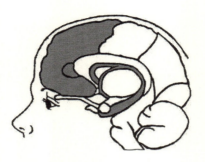

Frontal Cortex, Broca's Area,
Hippocampus

First, let's look at the frontal cortex. Located in the frontal lobe, this is the part of the brain where most of our conscious awareness is centered, and we depend heavily on this area to run our everyday lives. The frontal cortex needs to be working properly for us to be able to speak, to be alert, to be focused, and to be rational. Most of our bodily functions are affected by what happens here as chemicals produced in this area control metabolism, blood pressure, body temperature, energy levels, sleep, and motor control.

There are many factors that can negatively impact the operation of the frontal cortex including stress, poor nutrition, inadequate sleep, and drug and/or alcohol abuse. When processes in the frontal cortex are disrupted, the problems we may experience include:

1. The inability to focus and concentrate
2. Feeling so overwhelmed that we are unable to function
3. Anxiety that leaves us feeling scattered and unable to finish simple tasks
4. Feeling apathetic, insecure, and unmotivated to succeed
5. The inability to make decisions
6. Difficulties with self-expression and self-awareness
7. Explosive anger
8. Self-destructive thoughts and actions, including suicidal gestures
9. The need to people-please in an attempt to receive love and attention
10. Poor impulse control

The frontal cortex appears to be under the influence of the Broca's area which, I believe, is the will. Time and time again, I have seen how the Broca's area affects the overall operation of the entire frontal brain—even to the point that it can undermine an otherwise functioning frontal lobe. This shows us the power of the will. When the will is submitted to God, He can direct it to help us lead God-centered lives. A strong, God-directed will can stabilize frontal cortical functions while a weak or compromised will can disrupt them. The following example illustrates this point.[2]

Carl Learns How to Retrain His Will and His Mind

Carl came to see me because he had recently been hired to pastor a small church, but he was struggling in his new role. It appeared that Carl's frontal cortex was operating in faith, but because his will was weak, his faith-based perspective would periodically be overrun by his emotions. This caused him to make spiritual decisions based on how he felt rather than on what the Word of God says or what he knew to be right. Even though Carl was a dynamic speaker and a very compassionate individual, his leadership skills were lacking due to his weak will.

Through my work with him, I learned that Carl's childhood home had been very volatile, and emotions were allowed to run wild. His parents would yell and scream at each other and, occasionally, at their kids. Because he had never learned how to control his emotions as a child, he was still struggling with them as an adult.

To teach his brain to correct itself, I gave Carl exercises that focused on retraining both his will and his mind. These exercises are listed at the end of this chapter to help those of you dealing with similar issues.

---

[2] All examples in this book are of clients I have seen in my clinical practice. However, names and other details have been changed to protect their identities.

Though the frontal cortex houses much of our intellectual skills including reasoning, planning, organizing, sorting, self-expression, etc., it does not work alone. It works in conjunction with the hippocampus—the area of the brain that I refer to as the mind. The hippocampus is located in the limbic system in the temporal lobe. This region of the brain also contains the areas to which we are referring when we talk about the soul, the spirit, the heart, and our desires. These areas will be covered later, but for now I'd like to focus on the mind.

The hippocampus is responsible for guiding the entire brain in its cognitive functioning. Thus it has the ability to affect the frontal cortex and all the other parts of the brain that control behavior. In addition, memories are stored in the hippocampus and used there to form our belief systems that are later used to shape our value systems. This is why Solomon said that "as a man thinketh in his heart, so is he."

Because the hippocampus is such a critical area of the brain, it needs to be sound, strong, and efficient—free from interruptions and from negative and destructive patterns of thinking, interpreting, and believing. This is the reason so many preachers and authors focus on the mind in their teaching and preaching. We must observe 2 Corinthians 10:5 which states, "We demolish arguments and every pretension that sets itself up against the knowledge of God, and we take captive every thought to make it obedient to Christ."

Though there are others, the nine most common problems of the hippocampus (mind) are:

1. Distorted thinking that causes us to perceive reality inaccurately
2. Negative and destructive beliefs—for example, people believing they are bad or evil based on what their past experiences tell them—commonly referred to in Christian circles as lies
3. Emotional thinking which dramatically decreases our critical thinking abilities
4. Lustful and other ungodly thoughts
5. Disjointed thinking—the inability to string together continuous threads of ideas
6. Self-condemning and judgmental thoughts
7. Suicidal and other self-harming thoughts

8. Hateful and harming thoughts towards others
9. A worldly value system incompatible with Scripture

So what can you do if you struggle with one or more of these nine common problems in thinking? First, you need to ascertain if your issues are caused by a direct attack from the enemy. I will briefly present how to deal with enemy attacks in a later chapter.[3] However, since most of these kinds of problems stem from past experiences that influence our thinking and beliefs, one of the key things you need to do to manage this area is to deal with any past traumas you may have experienced. How do you go about this? The following example should prove helpful.

Randy Overcomes His Erroneous Thinking About God's Love

Randy, a 30-year-old Christian man, came to see me because he couldn't seem to shake the belief that God did not love him as much as He loves others. In his perspective, his friends received blessings upon blessings while in his own life nothing seemed to go his way. He also believed God could be punishing him for things he had done when he was younger. Randy attended church regularly, rarely missed church activities, and gave money to the church in the hope that he would be financially blessed. But none of these things seemed to make a difference in the circumstances of his life.

Randy was letting the way he felt dictate what he believed. He needed to look back at his past and learn what negative experiences had caused him to develop his erroneous beliefs, process those experiences, and retrain his brain to recognize and believe the truth. In this case, Randy's father favored his older brother over him, so I encouraged Randy to reeducate his mind by telling himself something like this:

---

[3] For a more comprehensive presentation of this topic, let me recommend my book on spiritual warfare, *Arming Your Brain with the Armor of God*, and my DVD, *Defeating Darkness*.

My father may have favored my big brother and showered him with gifts, but God is not like my father. Although it feels like God is doing what my father did, the truth is God loves me the same way He does other believers.

Many of us, like Randy, struggle with negative beliefs. These beliefs have developed because we've had trouble letting go of past painful experiences for which we hold God responsible. We may believe that God is distant, especially if our own fathers were distant. If our fathers didn't care, we may believe that God doesn't care. If our fathers were punitive, we may believe that God is punitive. If our fathers were performance-oriented, we may believe that God is performance-oriented. These beliefs can be resolved by first processing the experiences on which they're founded and then by learning the truth about God. At our clinic, we have found the following exercise helpful for clients who struggle with this kind of faulty thinking.

Creating a Scripture Collage

For this exercise, find 12 Scriptures about the attributes of God and put them in a grid like the one below. If you like, you can use a Bible concordance or search engine. Then read them out loud while asking God to make them real to your brain. You must read them yourself and not rely on a helper.

Scripture Collage Grid

Your negative and distorted beliefs may not be about God; they may be self, about others, and about the world. If that's the case, rather than choosing Scriptures about the character of God, look for Scriptures that apply to you, other people, or the world. This exercise is effective no matter what your distorted thinking is. The bottom line is that your brain needs to be fed what God says about reality and not what your experiences say.

Problems with thinking and beliefs affect the frontal cortex as well as the mind. The following case shows the kinds of problems that may result when the frontal areas of the brain are impacted by faulty thinking.

Dorothy Resolves Her Anxiety and Scattered Thinking and Behaviors

At the time Dorothy came to see me, she was in college and in danger of failing her classes because she couldn't concentrate on her schoolwork. She was a constant worrier, and she told her close friends that she had been full of worry and fear for as long as she could remember. In addition, many of her friends considered her to be scatterbrained because she started numerous projects but couldn't seem to finish them.

Dorothy grew up in a home where there was a lot of uncertainty. Her parents were constantly arguing and screaming at one another, at Dorothy, and at her brothers and sisters. This produced a great deal of fear and anxiety in Dorothy and her siblings. In fact, Dorothy's anxiety was so bad that she had to be put on anti-anxiety medication to help her get some breathing room so she could then focus on training her brain to function more efficiently.

Because Dorothy's inner brain was using energy to handle her fear issues, the front part of her brain was being deprived of the energy needed to deal with her everyday life. By helping her brain to process her traumatic memories, Dorothy was able to resolve her fear issues thus making more energy available to her front brain.

I gave Dorothy the following exercises to help her overcome problems in the frontal areas of the brain.

1. To help her to become less scatterbrained, I had Dorothy write out a schedule each day and follow it.
2. Because Dorothy needed to learn to think things through rather than become enmeshed in her feelings, I had her read stories and tell me what the characters in the stories were thinking. I then asked her to tell me what she thought about the stories she read. I specifically instructed her not to pay attention to her feelings or the feelings of the characters in the stories. This exercise increases activity in the frontal areas of the brain.

There are many people whose functioning deteriorates when they must focus undue energy on keeping down inner turmoil as a result of past traumas they experienced, as was the case with Dorothy. We all need to work through any past traumas that may be interfering with the quality of our lives.

In addition, there are practical things we can do to maintain the health of our minds and the other areas of the brain we rely on to function well on a daily basis. For example, the value of mental exercises has been well-documented. We also need to take care of our bodies through proper eating, good physical exercise, and plenty of sleep.

Our society does not rest or sleep well. We are up at night watching television or working on our computers. Then we don't want to get up in the morning, and we make mistakes at work or school because we've had insufficient sleep. Our frontal lobes do not function well when we have not gotten sufficient rest. And our eating habits are not much better. We need to eat foods that provide our minds with the quality fuel they need to work well.

Chapter 3

Managing Your Perceptions

For the word of God is alive and active. Sharper than any double-edged sword, it penetrates even to dividing soul and spirit, joints and marrow; it judges the thoughts and attitudes of the heart.

Hebrews 4:12

Our brains receive information through our five senses of touch, smell, sight, taste, and hearing, and we use this information to interpret our environment and draw conclusions that affect our understanding of ourselves and the world around us. This is perception. The areas of the brain involved in perception work together with the reasoning sections of the brain.

The importance of perception is obvious. It has tremendous impact on our overall knowledge and understanding. It influences what we do with the information we receive and how we apply what we learn. We should allow God's Word—which Hebrews 4:12 tells us is alive, active, and powerful—to color our perceptions. Then anything that comes into our brains will be screened correctly, and our perceptions will be less skewed.

We all perceive things differently. Two people can be looking at a cloud in the sky, and one perceives it as a woman holding a child while the other perceives it as a woman riding a bike. There are two possible reasons for this phenomenon. First, our unique past experiences impact the way we see things, and second, our brains may process images differently.

There may be biological influences that affect how we perceive. For example, sensory processing disorder is a new term we use in the mental health field. SPD fits in the category of developmental disorders: a group of psychiatric conditions that interrupt normal development in childhood. When a child has this disorder, his or her brain is not able to handle certain sensory input normally. A child with sensory processing disorder may get very upset by loud noises or shy away from being touched because his or her sense of touch is easily overloaded. Another child with SPD may struggle with handling emotions and be easily overwhelmed by them.

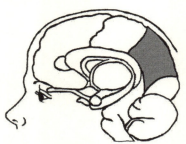

Perception Part of the
Parietal Lobe

The parietal lobe is associated with perception and relationality. It produces chemicals that help our brains to be creative, and this creativity is used to help us to perceive and to relate. When we have problems in this area, we may struggle with relationships, self-esteem, and identity.

Issues concerning relationships and identity will be covered in a later chapter. Now let's look at the problem of distorted perceptions. The following list contains examples of perceptual problems therapists commonly observe in their clients.

1. Perceiving the world to be against them
2. Perceiving other people to be there to hurt them
3. Perceiving life to be hard and unpleasant
4. Perceiving all women to be controlling
5. Perceiving all men to be abusive
6. Perceiving God to be uncaring and unloving
7. Perceiving marriage to be nothing but a source of pain
8. Perceiving specific people to be incapable of change

Most of these kinds of distortions stem from past experiences that continue to color our current realities. If we want to be able to change our distorted perceptions, we need to let go of those past experiences. We need to change our filtering systems. If our filtering systems are filled with negative and painful experiences, our chances of perceiving healthily are slim.

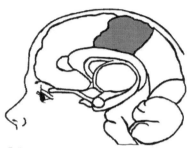

Motor and Sensory Cortex

The area of the brain with the most impact on our perceptions about the world is the motor and sensory cortex of the parietal lobe. This is where the earliest lessons we learned as very small children have the greatest bearing. If we experienced the world as safe and secure, and if our families provided us with love, acceptance, and value, chances are we will perceive the world around us in normal ways. This is why good parenting is so important. The choices parents make in their children's formative years can influence their perceptions throughout their lives.

Though we can't go back and change the past experiences that produced our distorted perceptions, we can discover what those experiences taught us, let go of our false conclusions, and then train our brains in new and different ways of perceiving. The following examples will help you to understand how.

Adolphus Resolves His Fear-based
Perception of the World

Adolphus didn't trust anyone. He thought that everyone was out to get him. He was afraid of other men and avoided male relationships. He preferred spending time with women yet wouldn't let any one woman get close to him. Many people described him as the most negative person they knew. For example, when a friend of his excitedly told Adolphus that his girlfriend was going to have a baby, Adolphus declared that it was a bad idea to bring an innocent child into this cruel world.

It seemed clear to me that Adolphus was speaking from his own negative childhood experiences—which his brain map confirmed. He had grown up with an abusive father who often beat him. His mother was the only real parent he had, but unfortunately, she over-bonded with him, and he felt totally controlled by her. I knew that if Adolphus didn't resolve his issues, he might never marry or have children. He would likely live a life of loneliness.

The first thing he needed to do was to deal with the trauma inflicted by his parents. Then he could train his brain in a new way of perceiving the world. The process wasn't easy, but it worked.

Next I had Adolphus construct a collage of pictures showing how he thought about his world. After discussing the images he had put on his collage and helping him process what they meant to him, I had Adolphus make a collage of what he wanted his world to be like. This activity began to train his brain to conceive of a new reality that was more conducive to a positive view of life. Over time, his brain was able to embrace this reality.

You would be amazed to know how much negative perceptions influence a person's future. Truly, you can change your whole outlook on life by changing the way you perceive, and by changing your outlook on life, you can change your current—and future—life experiences.

We have all heard it said that perception is everything. A common example is the concept that a person will consider a glass that is half filled to be either half empty or half full depending on whether his or her perceptual outlook is positive or negative. Those who tend to "see the glass as half empty" experience life very differently than those who tend to "see the glass as half full." Therein lies the power of perception.

Another way to resolve our negative perceptions is to deliberately focus on the good points of our experiences rather than on the bad points. Through the counseling process, Betty learned to do this with her perspective on marriage.

Betty Changes Her View on Marriage

At 54, Betty had been married four times and had given up on the idea of ever marrying again. Her experiences with marriage had been heartbreaking, and she didn't want to put herself—or another man—through that kind of pain once more. It was surprising to me that Betty didn't blame the men in her past for her marriage woes. She took sole responsibility, believing she just wasn't capable of being in a marriage.

Betty's brain map revealed severe sexual abuse in her past, which she confirmed. She had been sexually abused by a number of men: some of them relatives and some drug abusers with whom her mother had been involved. Betty had spent no time with her father. He left when she was a small girl and never came back to see her.

Betty recognized that the severe sexual abuse and the abandonment by her father led her to seek a father's love instead of marital love. Thus she chose to marry much older men who soon became disappointed by her immature behavior.

Betty needed to work through both the traumas of sexual abuse and of abandonment. Through her counseling sessions, Betty learned that the sexual abuse had affected what she believed about sex, love, attention, and affection. She mistakenly thought that the attention many men gave her meant that they loved her. Sleeping with them was her way of expressing love to them, but it became confusing for her when she was having a sexual relationship with more than one man at the same time. Betty had to learn to separate the concepts of paternal love and marital love to be able to view love and marriage correctly. Finally, Betty began to see that it was not too late for her to have a different experience of marriage than she had in the past.

Betty was fortunate that she was able to work through her past experiences so that they will no longer influence her perspective in a negative way going forward. So many people get stuck in their negativity and continue to struggle to adopt a positive view. This is particularly detrimental when it comes to the perception of God.

Since Christians are not exempt from problems throughout life, even we can struggle with our understanding of God. Though we're saved, we still need to grow in our knowledge of Him and become more and more like Christ as we do. This is a process that involves learning about Him and experiencing Him first-hand in our lives. Since we may develop perception problems from our very earliest life experiences, we likely had issues in our perception areas of the brain before we became Christians. If so, we most likely still have those issues, and it will take work and time to resolve them.

There are some basic perceptual problems concerning God that both counselors and preachers hear from people they help. The biggest misconception involves how God relates to us. There are many people who perceive Him as being very distant and uninvolved in our lives. Their belief in an impersonal God leads them to feel uncared for by Him and gives them no reason to entrust their lives to Him.

This perception seems to be rooted in the way God was first presented to them. If God was presented as being far away and impersonal; more interested in the universe and Himself than in them; or too big, busy, and important to care about them as individuals; it's understandable why they struggle to see Him as desiring a personal relationship with them.

This perception about God is also rooted in people's relationships with their fathers. It's commonly known that people's views of their earthly fathers color their views of our Heavenly Father. Therefore, fathers, take note. You can help influence your children to have a healthy perception of God. If you are warm, open, and close to your children, you will help them perceive God as warm, communicative, and relational. If, however, you are harsh, punitive, and judgmental, your children may perceive God to be so as well. If you communicate to your children that you are too busy to have time for them, they may come to believe that God is too busy for them too or that they are not important enough for Him to give them personal attention.

You can see how our experiences color our perceptions and, at times, distort reality. We Christians, especially, need to be careful not to allow our experiences to color our understanding of God. The problem is exacerbated when doctrines and teachings in the church are based on experiences rather than truth. Though our experiences may change, truth never does. Though our experiences vary from person to person, the truth about God remains the same. Truth can influence how we feel, but how we feel should not be allowed to influence our understanding of truth. Our experiences should be anchored in truth, but truth should not be anchored on our experiences.

Chapter 4

Managing Your Emotions

The thief comes only to steal and kill and destroy; I have come that they may have life, and have it to the full.

John 10:10

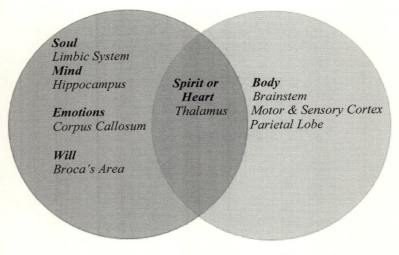

Soul
Limbic System
Mind
Hippocampus

Emotions
Corpus Callosum

Will
Broca's Area

Spirit or
Heart
Thalamus

Body
Brainstem
Motor & Sensory Cortex
Parietal Lobe

Diagram of the Relationship Between the
Inner Man and the Outer Man in the Brain

You can find varying views on emotions and their value, but the important thing to know is that emotions are good and necessary for us to be able to experience life to the fullest. We need emotions connecting our "inner man" to our "outer man," so to speak. In my view, the parts of the brain we rely on for everyday functioning, relating to the world around us, and our perception of that world are what constitute the outer man. The illustration on the previous page shows how those areas of the brain connect with the areas comprising the inner man.

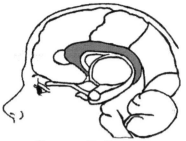

Corpus Callosum

According to my research, emotions are best utilized when they are in the corpus callosum because from there all of the functioning brain can have access to them. We need an emotional component to our everyday life experiences. If emotions are removed from them, life becomes mechanical, and we no longer feel like we're living but, rather, are just going through the motions.

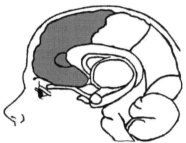

Frontal Cortex

It is good when emotions are available to the frontal areas of the brain. The problem comes when the frontal lobe is run by emotions. When this happens, we may become overly emotional at inappropriate times or be easily overwhelmed. In addition, emotions in the frontal brain, especially in the Broca's area, can lead to problems with decision-making. We may become indecisive or our emotions may cause us to make poor decisions.

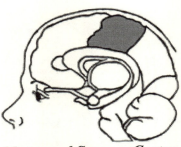

Motor and Sensory Cortex

The motor and sensory cortex also needs a connection to emotions but, again, should not be overrun by them. This area of the brain is involved with how we take in information through our five senses of sight, taste, smell, touch, and hearing, and all our senses depend on emotions to engage fully.

My research suggests that we heavily rely on this area of the brain to relate to one another. Relating, in its most basic definition, is giving information to others and receiving information from them. But our interactions with one another are multi-faceted, and certainly, emotions are a big component of them. Balance is key. Both too much emotion and too little emotion can lead to instability in relationships. I have counseled a number of married couples who were emotionally out of balance. One spouse related emotionally and, as a result, was overly sensitive, while the other related factually with little emotion. For balance in this area, emotions need to be in the corpus callosum rather than in the motor and sensory cortex.

The motor and sensory cortex is also involved in perception. Though perception was covered in the previous chapter, here I want to specifically address the important role of emotions in perception. Because this area of the brain appears to be particularly involved with self-perception, too much emotion here can skew the way an individual perceives him- or herself. Such people may identify themselves as weak and overly emotional. Their self-perception tends to shift constantly leading to instability.

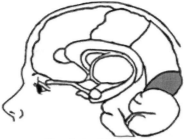

Occipital Lobe

Our outlook on life, motivation and drive, and the ability to forecast into the future are all functions of the visual cortex in the occipital lobe. You can imagine what too much emotion, and the resulting instability it may produce, can do to these functions. Though our emotions are valid, they do not always tell us the truth. Therefore, they cannot be trusted to guide us into the future or provide us with the necessary motivation to achieve.

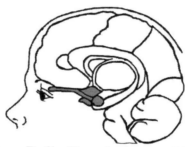

Olfactory Bulb, Hypothalamus, Pituitary

The last section of the brain I want to address in relation to emotions is the olfactory area which includes the olfactory bulb, the hypothalamus, the pituitary gland, and the amygdala. I call this area the emergency response system of the brain.

In brain science literature, the olfactory bulb is reported to be associated with the sense of smell, but through my research I have found the olfactory bulb to be correlated with all the five senses. This is understandable as we need all our senses involved in order for us to respond to emergencies effectively.

When something is emotionally threatening, the olfactory bulb sends this information to the amygdala. As the alarm of the brain, the amygdala sounds a warning to the parts of the brain that control behavior so the appropriate actions can be taken. The amygdala then sends a message to the pituitary and adrenal glands to produce the chemicals the body needs to respond to the emergency. These chemicals are necessary when the body needs a "fight or flight" response to a real physical threat. However, the body has nothing to combat physically in the case of emotional threat, yet the chemicals are still released into the blood stream causing stress and other emotionally upsetting symptoms. This is what happens when someone has an anxiety or panic attack.

In addition, too much emotion in the amygdala can result in false alarms. This seems to be what happens when trauma victims react to a current situation based on a past traumatic experience and erroneously believe the experience is happening all over again. I often tell my trauma clients that the amygdala does not know the difference between the past and the present.

Too much emotion in the hypothalamus can have powerful repercussions. This area performs the critical job of regulating sleep, eating, drinking, sex drive, and pain and pleasure tolerance. You can imagine the disruption to our everyday lives if emotions overwhelm the hypothalamus.

You can see why it's important for this entire area to be functioning well in order for us to respond to emotional emergencies in a stable and efficient manner. Too much emotion in the emergency response system predisposes people to overreactions whenever there is a perceived threat.

We all want to know how to handle our emotions so that they don't handle us. Let me emphasize again that emotions are good and necessary, but we don't want them taking over our cognitive functions. Therefore, we want to make sure they are centered in the appropriate area of the brain. The following example shows how Gerald learned to put his emotions in their proper place.

Gerald Regains His Functioning
Skills and Saves His Job

Gerald, a 45-year-old manager at a computer company, often exhibited immature behavior. When he was doing well, he would happily spend time with his customers helping them with problems and showing them how to play certain games on their computers. But when things weren't going well and he was confronted, he would blow up and threaten to quit. Gerald's boss perceived him as undisciplined, unmotivated, and lacking aspirations to move up in the company. When Gerald came in for help, he was on the brink of losing his job.

Through a brain evaluation, I learned that Gerald was a highly emotional guy. His emotions affected his cognitive and relational functions and drove his aspirations and outlook on life. As a result, these things fluctuated and were unstable.

In the weeks that followed, I helped Gerald understand why he struggled to control his emotions. As a child, he had been spoiled by his parents, and they never required him to learn self-control. His emotions were allowed free reign; consequently, they dominated every area of his brain.

Though Gerald had always perceived his childhood as wonderful, he soon realized that the fact that he had been spoiled left him emotionally crippled. When he embarked on a journey of healing his childhood experiences, he found he had a lot of angry feelings he had to work through. It was a painful process for him to have to learn to control his emotions and to exercise the cognitive areas of his brain without allowing them to be overrun by his feelings.

The following exercises helped Gerald to regain his cognitive functions.

1. When making a decision, Gerald was asked to write down the process he used and give the reasons for his decision. Doing so repeatedly helped retrain his brain to think rather than emote.
2. I gave Gerald specific examples of people working from their emotions. His assignment was to write out rational ways the individuals in each case could have handled their situations.

3. I encouraged Gerald to go back in his mind to circumstances in which he had reacted emotionally and come up with rational alternative responses.
4. After concluding each of these calculative and rational exercises, Gerald was also encouraged to experience and express his emotions.

These exercises are very effective for anyone with problems similar to Gerald's. Those who identify with Maud's situation will find the approach she took to her behavior and relating problems helpful.

Maud Overcomes Her Unhealthy
Behaviors and Ways of Relating

Maud's husband complained that he always had to walk on eggshells around her. The 36-year-old mother of three readily admitted that she was often a basket case. Everyone around her had been telling her she was too sensitive and easily hurt. Her husband was especially tired of her crying over every little thing that went wrong. In a way, Maud related to him as if he were her father rather than her husband, and he had to admit that with Maud he sometimes felt like he was dealing with a child. Even her kids thought their mom was not strong enough to handle anything. Maud was understandably distraught about her situation and felt she didn't deserve to be a wife or mother.

Maud's brain map showed that her motor and sensory cortex was overrun with emotion. This is what was primarily responsible for her broken boundaries with people that were making it easy for others to control her and hurt her emotionally.

Like most people with relational issues, Maud's early childhood interpersonal experiences were at the heart of her problems. Maud was always regarded as a weakling by her family. Consequently, she was over-protected and never given any hard tasks to complete. Though she was told she was too emotional, nothing was ever done to help her build up her intellect and to redirect her excess emotions away from her cognitive functions.

The following steps helped Maud to work through her issues.

1. Maud had to learn to grieve and forgive the things that happened in her life when she was growing up. As she gained a better understanding of herself and began letting go of her childhood issues, Maud's brain was given the opportunity to start maturing so it could catch up to her chronological age.
2. Maud had to change the very strong beliefs about relating that were driving her behavior. Here are Maud's beliefs, which are common to people with these kinds of problems.

- *If I am emotional and cry easily, people will be kind to me and meet my needs.* This belief was established and reinforced by Maud's parents. When Maud would become emotional and cry, her parents rewarded her by jumping to her rescue instead of helping her work through the situation she was facing. Maud needed to learn to accept the fact that bad things happen, face the difficulties she encountered, and stand up on her own rather than simply fold.

- *I am weak and unable to do much for myself, so other people need to do things for me.* This belief is what caused Maud to be overly dependent on her parents (especially her father) as a child and on her husband as an adult. Unfortunately, an adult who is overly reliant on another person is more vulnerable to being hurt by that person. Maud had to learn to limit her dependence on others. This slowly brought her personal strength, power, and control until she was no longer always at the mercy of others.

- *It's okay for others to be strong and independent, but it's wrong for me.* Maud thought that God created her to be an emotional person. This was a difficult thing for her to work through in therapy. First, we know that God makes each of us uniquely different. There is no doubt that Maud's emotional nature is part of God's design for her. But Maud's poor upbringing led to the over-development of her emotional side and the under-development of her rational side.

Clearly, Maud's over-emotionalism made her—and her whole family—miserable. I helped Maud understand that God gave her emotions so that she could enjoy her life: her husband, her kids, her friends, and her activities. He did not intend for those emotions to bring her misery. This is true for you too if you struggle with this same issue. Whatever your predisposition, remember that when it starts giving you problems, it's no longer working as God intended.

- *Emotional people are better than non-emotional people.* It's easy to see how someone can believe this. Non-emotional people are often out of touch with the feelings of others and can, therefore, easily ignore other people's pain. However, though they may have a problem allowing themselves to experience their emotions, that doesn't make them any worse than individuals who are overrun with emotions. The issue here is not predisposition; the issue is how emotions are managed.

Maud learned that she could help manage her emotions by strengthening her thinking. She used the exercises for managing thinking covered in chapter 2 of this book to help her balance her emotions and her cognitions.

Chapter 5

Managing Your Reactions

His divine power has given us everything we need for a godly life through our knowledge of him who called us by his own glory and goodness. Through these he has given us his very great and precious promises, so that through them you may participate in the divine nature, having escaped the corruption in the world caused by evil desires.

For this very reason, make every effort to add to your faith goodness; and to goodness, knowledge; and to knowledge, self-control; and to self-control, perseverance; and to perseverance, godliness; and to godliness, mutual affection; and to mutual affection, love. For if you possess these qualities in increasing measure, they will keep you from being ineffective and unproductive in your knowledge of our Lord Jesus Christ. But whoever does not have them is nearsighted and blind, forgetting that they have been cleansed from their past sins.

II Peter 1:3-9

Though I briefly touched on reactions in the previous chapter, I feel it's important to address this topic specifically. The areas in the brain associated with reactionary behaviors are those involved with emotional responses along with the motor and sensory cortex.

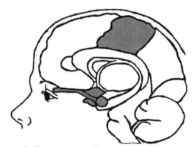

Motor and Sensory Cortex, Olfactory Area

Now that you understand how the emergency response system of the brain works, let's look at how it interacts with the relational area of the brain. The motor and sensory cortex, which acts as the gateway into the brain, manages how we receive and present information when we relate to others. These interactions occur in a variety of ways. Obviously, we are aware of how we interact with others through words, gestures, and actions on a conscious level, but it is well known that we also communicate with one another on a subconscious level through things like body language, eye movement, vocal inflection, and other intuitive signals we give off and pick up from others.

All our interactions need to occur in balanced and healthy ways, but when we have problems in the motor and sensory cortex, we are more likely to relate in dysfunctional ways. Fear and anxiety may take over leading us to close up and shut people out. We may become hard and angry as a way to protect ourselves. Or, rather than closing ourselves off to others, we may become way too open in an attempt to get our needs met, and as a result, we may become overly sensitive, resort to people-pleasing, or become so clingy that others feel we are sucking the life from them in our relationships. We may also become super-controlling and demanding—even using religion to control others—as a way to stay safe.

When the brain goes into survival mode and turns to the emergency response system for help in a non-emergency situation, things can quickly spiral out of control. Everything becomes intensified, and destructive modes of coping take over. Stella's situation before she came for therapy is a perfect example of this.

Stella Overcomes Her Addictions to Food, Sex, and Relationships

The men in 30-year-old Stella's church singles' group knew that she dated around and slept with a lot of guys. Those who had dated her didn't like how clingy and needy she was. Her girlfriends called her a relationship junky. Whenever she broke up with a guy, she became almost frantic to get in another relationship to avoid being alone. Stella also struggled with her weight. Each year she made a New Year's resolution to lose the weight, but she wasn't able to stay on a diet and exercise program.

Stella's brain map revealed her abandonment issues. Because she had been deserted by her father, she was always looking for a man to fill that gap. In addition, his abandonment had caused her relational brain to shut down. Since the need for a relationship was critical to her, Stella had begun relating from her emergency response area of the brain. This made it difficult for her to seek out and sustain healthy relationships. In the area of the brain that registers addiction, Stella also showed addiction to relationships as well as to food and sex.

I helped Stella understand what was happening in her brain to cause her to struggle with these issues. She had known that she used sex to experience closeness and affection and that her eating was for comfort because she ate when she felt lonely. Still, she hadn't realized just how much the pain of abandonment had been driving her need for love, affection, and comfort and affecting her choices in these matters.

When Stella was ready, we addressed the trauma caused by the abandonment. Walking through it was difficult for her, but Stella felt it was worth it in the end. Afterward, she was able to learn proper ways of relating. As her relational brain began working better, and the emergency response system was relieved, Stella had fewer problems with the addictions that had troubled her.

The emergency response system of the brain is for emergencies only and not for everyday relating. Reactions in this area of the brain are normal when we are under a threat—that's how we are wired to survive—but they should be occasional. It's a real problem when reactions become a way to cope. We should be acting, not reacting.

Following are the 4 most universal types of unhealthy reactions. If you can master dealing with them, you will be able to apply the same principles to overcome any reaction issues with which you may struggle.

1. Fear-based reactions are probably the most common ones. They occur when the emergency response system of the brain misinterprets a perceived threat and responds to it as if it is an actual one. This perceived threat is reported as real to the entire brain, and the body answers with a physiological response. Chemicals are released into the blood stream, but there is no physical situation for which they are needed.

Sometimes the body is actually harmed by these chemical reactions—such as when they produce ulcers, panic attacks, and other psychosomatic problems. I believe there are a lot of people who complain of physical illnesses who are actually experiencing a chemical response to emotional troubles that go unresolved.

I am not the only mental health professional who feels that our culture puts too much emphasis on the physical and not enough on the emotional and mental. Our society has divided our health problems into two different categories—major medical and mental health. The major medical category is obviously viewed as the more important one. Insurance companies pay more for major medical issues than they do for mental health issues, and many companies that provide major medical benefits for their employees do not also provide mental health benefits.

This approach to health care isn't scientifically sound since our brains house and marry both the physical and emotional areas of our lives. In fact, research has shown that our emotional and mental states have power over the physical and, consequently, the medical issues we may face (though medical issues can, in turn, make emotional and mental problems worse). For example, many sleep difficulties as well as thyroid and endocrine issues are the result of unresolved fear and anxiety. Our tendency as a nation to throw medications at everything makes this problem worse because then our brains don't learn to resolve the reasons behind the issues.

2. Next, let's look at anxiety-based reactions. These are not the same as fear-based reactions, as fear and anxiety are differentiated in the brain. Those with anxiety issues experience fear, but usually the fear isn't about any specific thing. In addition, people with anxiety are afraid of things that are not there.

Anxiety-based reactions include worry, lack of trust, and absence of peace. People with anxiety disorders often have an inner restlessness that makes it difficult for them to sleep, and they usually exhibit a variety of physical symptoms as well. Anxiety can keep people trapped in a type of prison in their minds. It teaches them not to trust others or get too close to them, and it makes it difficult for them to believe in the goodness of God.

3. Now let's look at emotion-based reactions. Remember, the way we react in an emergency can be critical to our survival. We can't afford to have our emotions ruling in those situations because emotions do not think. When the emergency area of the brain is flooded with emotions, our reactions are determined by those emotions. For example, a person who feels threatened may strike at someone who is actually trying to help. We can't make wise decisions when we are overwhelmed with feelings. We need cool, clear heads to determine the best and safest ways to react.

4. Finally, let's look at a specific—and common—emotion-based reaction: the anger-based reaction. Anger-based reactions can be very destructive. You have probably heard it said that anger usually covers up hurt. Anger fuels the brain with the desire to inflict pain on those who have hurt us or to strike out in order to protect us from being hurt any further. Anger may even lead us to embrace evil if it appears that doing so will help our situation. Though anger is normally employed in an attempt at self-protection, it can also be turned inward causing people to hurt themselves—even to the point of suicide.

People who have been physically and/or verbally abused or severely neglected often develop these anger-based reactions. I have also found anger-based reactions to be common in adult children of alcoholics.

So how do we deal with these unhealthy reactions? Let's look at how Jessie and Tessa managed theirs.

Jessie Overcomes His Anger-based Reactions

When Jessie became my client, he was a twenty-five-year-old man who had lost most of his friends because of his angry outbursts. His girlfriend, Tessa, had recently broken up with him because he was yelling at her and, at times, hitting her.

Jessie had grown up in a home where there was constant yelling and fighting between his mother and father. After many years, Jessie's mom had grown tired of the fighting and had left Jessie's dad. Jessie had told himself he would never be like his father, but as he got older he was actually becoming more and more like him.

Because of his background, Jessie struggled with the fear of being rejected and abandoned. Whenever he did something wrong, his fear that Tessa would leave him caused him to take his feelings out on her, his work associates, and his friends. Jessie was using his anger to cover the hurts he carried in his heart. Unfortunately, his angry outbursts were having the opposite effect.

Facing his abusive past allowed Jessie's brain to empty itself of the bad memories from his childhood. Next Jessie needed to realize that he wasn't the monster he had believed himself to be because of his struggles with negative behaviors and feelings. Jessie learned to be vulnerable with safe people, to open up about his hurts, and to stop always playing the tough guy.

Tessa Overcomes Her Fear-based Reactions

Tessa, Jessie's girlfriend, came with him to one of his sessions with me and, after breaking up with him, returned for some sessions of her own. Tessa is a beautiful young woman who had been attracted to Jessie because he appeared to be strong and fearless. She assumed he would protect her, but she also confessed that she had always been attracted to "bad boys." Tessa's friends were often puzzled by this because Tessa seemed to be stable and intelligent. What they didn't know was that her father had a temper, and she had grown up used to yelling and screaming.

But Tessa's particular experience with an angry father was different from most. After an angry outburst, Tessa's father would always apologize and be extra sweet and nice toward his daughter. For Tessa, this established a belief that after a guy is angry or abusive toward you, he will be contrite and solicitous to make up for his poor behavior. So each time Jessie would explode at her, Tessa would hope that he would do what her father had done. But he never did.

Helping Tessa became easier once she came to understand that her issues in her relationship with Jessie were a direct result of her past experiences with her father. Tessa worked through her trauma from both her father and Jessie and began to learn proper boundaries in her relationships.

The principles given here to help with anger- and fear-based reactions can be used to help with reactions in general. Another way to mitigate reactions of all types is through the use of Scripture to reframe and redirect unhealthy coping mechanisms. For example, when a person has an anxious personality, outlook, or relational style, he or she can make a Scripture collage as illustrated in chapter 2. This exercise is geared toward confronting the issues in the brain and allowing the Scriptures to correct the beliefs causing the problems. It has proven to be an amazing tool, always pinpointing the specific area of the brain that needs the exact message in each Scripture chosen.

We all have had the experience of dealing with someone who is reactionary, and it's not fun. You can't reason with reactionary people. They are often unpredictable, and it's difficult to know the best way to handle them. If you are a reactionary person, you can recognize the importance of gaining control of the problematic areas of your brain. Remember, we are to exhibit the qualities of faith, goodness, knowledge, self-control, perseverance, godliness, mutual affection, and love; but when we are controlled by our reactions, we are in danger of being like those who are "nearsighted and blind, forgetting that they have been cleansed from their past sins." (2 Peter 1:9)

Chapter 6

Managing Your Identity

So God created the great creatures of the sea and every living thing with which the water teems and that moves about in it, according to their kinds, and every winged bird according to its kind. And God saw that it was good.

Genesis 1:21

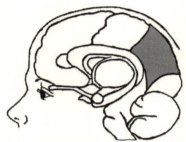

Perception Part of the Parietal Lobe

Although every chapter in this book is important, this chapter is a crucial one when it comes to the subject of managing your brain and your life because your identity is central to all that you do. Not knowing who you are will greatly diminish your experience of life: what you chose to do and how you function, relate, perceive, think, behave, and react.

So, who are you? What is your true identity? Do others define your identity for you? Is your identity tied in with your job, your looks, your fortune, or fame? Are you happy with who you are? Do you have more than one identity? So really, who do you believe you are? I'm sure you will agree this question is not an easy one to answer.

There are many books written on self-esteem and related topics, but do they really tell us what identity is? In this chapter, I will address the questions concerning identity using my research on the brain.

The first thing I discovered is that most of what we call identity is actually *perceived* identity. Perceived identity is heavily influenced by how we were raised and our circumstances; therefore, the perceived identity area of the brain varies from person to person. True identity, on the other hand, doesn't change and has nothing to do with our experiences or our perceptions.

We define our creations; they don't define themselves. It is the same with man and his Maker. This may sound very simplistic, but your true identity rests with God. God has the final say on who you are. But if you are like most people, you have let your upbringing and your experiences tell you who you are, and these things do not, and cannot, define your identity. In fact, God has already declared who you are. Though all the resources were there when the idea of your existence was born in the heart of God, only God the Father, God the Son, and God the Holy Spirit were present. So what does the Triune God have to say about your identity?

> Then God said, "Let us make mankind in our image, in our likeness, so that they may rule over the fish in the sea and the birds in the sky, over the livestock and all the wild animals, and over all the creatures that move along the ground.
>
> So God created mankind in his own image, in the image of God he created them; male and female he created them.
>
> Genesis 1:26-27

According to the truth of Scripture, your identity and mine are in God because we were created in His image. This means that questions of value and purpose tied to identity rest with God, not us. The fact that the Almighty God of the Universe put that much thought in making us in his image and likeness should tell us a lot about how He feels about us. God made us before we did anything; therefore, what we do, how we were raised, and all our experiences throughout our lives have no bearing on who we are. So if you want to improve your self-image, you will do yourself a great service by paying attention to what God says about you. Notice I am not saying that being created in the image of God makes you equal with or the same as God. But it certainly means there is a family resemblance that should make you feel good about yourself.

The second thing I discovered about identity is that it is something the enemy loves to attack. From the fall of man, throughout human history, Satan has sought to do two things: to undermine God and to destroy humans. And what better way is there to try to destroy human beings than in the area of identity? It is the target of all psychological traumas. In all my almost forty years of dealing with traumatized people—whether as a pastor, evangelist, or clinician—that's the area I have seen take the biggest hit.

Look at Adam and Eve. When they listened to the serpent, they lost their understanding of who they really were. They had been happy and fellowshipping with God, but after succumbing to Satan's temptation, they carried the weight of sin and the sentence of death. Their shame led them to try to hide themselves and their nakedness. This had to be very traumatic for them. Can you imagine trying to cover yourself with leaves?

As our adversary, Satan desires our harm and always will, whether we realize it or not. And the fact that we were actually made in God's image makes him hate us all the more. Therefore, we need to protect ourselves from him—especially in this area. For you, that may need to begin with healing your identity.

The third thing I discovered about identity is that, despite what people might believe, it can never be destroyed. However, it can be covered up or pushed down so far that we can live our lives never knowing our true identities. There are so many things the enemy uses to accomplish this—from physical and emotional trauma to sin and generational iniquities.

There is a great deal of confusion about identity as it relates to behavior. The truth is that there is no relationship between the two. As I said, God made us before we did anything; therefore, we are not what we do. Yes, our experiences can influence how we perceive ourselves, but perceived identity is unstable and should not be the basis for our understanding of who we are. If it is, when our experiences and circumstance change, then our understanding of who we are will change as well, and that is not a good thing. We are not our jobs, our looks, or our social status.

One day I left the office early and headed to a golf course to play a round of golf. There the clubhouse put me together with three other golfers. When we joined one another at the tee box, we all introduced ourselves using our first names only and shook hands. Soon after the introductions, as if to say our names were not enough information, the question arose as to what everyone did for a living.

The first player said he was a corporate lawyer; the next said he managed a software company. When my turn came, I declined to divulge any further information about myself, preferring to be identified only by my first name. The others seemed uncomfortable with this, jokingly wondering if I worked for the CIA or the IRS. I told the group that I had skipped out of the office early to have some fun and didn't want to mix business with pleasure.

I actually knew the fourth guy in our group. He worked at a school as the groundskeeper. But when he introduced himself, he said he worked in technical support for a school. I understood why this poor guy felt he had to come up with a more professional-sounding career. The other two men seemed to have such impressive resumés. At that point, I felt even more reticent to tell the group what I did for a living.

As we played along, the groundskeeper became more comfortable with me, and he confided that he had said he was in technical support because he was embarrassed to say what he actually did for a living in front of the rest of the group. The problem here is that the men had equated identity with what we do for a living.

We all know how commonly parents call their kids negative things when they get upset with them. They may call their child who is unmotivated to do his homework a "loser." Or they may say that their child who is always in trouble is a "bad seed." These words describe the child's behavior, but that is not who the child is: not his or her true identity. Unfortunately, these kinds of words influence the child's perceived identity.

One of my favorite stories in the gospels is that of the prodigal son. Most people know the story, but I have included it here for review.

Jesus continued: "There was a man who had two sons. The younger one said to his father, 'Father, give me my share of the estate.' So he divided his property between them.

"Not long after that, the younger son got together all he had, set off for a distant country and there squandered his wealth in wild living. After he had spent everything, there was a severe famine in that whole country, and he began to be in need. So he went and hired himself out to a citizen of that country, who sent him to his fields to feed pigs. He longed to fill his stomach with the pods that the pigs were eating, but no one gave him anything.

"When he came to his senses, he said, 'How many of my father's hired servants have food to spare, and here I am starving to death! I will set out and go back to my father and say to him: Father, I have sinned against heaven and against you. I am no longer worthy to be called your son; make me like one of your hired servants.' So he got up and went to his father.

"But while he was still a long way off, his father saw him and was filled with compassion for him; he ran to his son, threw his arms around him and kissed him.

"The son said to him, 'Father, I have sinned against heaven and against you. I am no longer worthy to be called your son.'

"But the father said to his servants, 'Quick! Bring the best robe and put it on him. Put a ring on his finger and sandals on his feet. Bring the fattened calf and kill it. Let's have a feast and celebrate. For this son of mine was dead and is alive again; he was lost and is found.' So they began to celebrate.

"Meanwhile, the older son was in the field. When he came near the house, he heard music and dancing. So he called one of the servants and asked him what was going on. 'Your brother has come,' he replied, 'and your father has killed the fattened calf because he has him back safe and sound.'

"The older brother became angry and refused to go in. So his father went out and pleaded with him. But he answered his father, 'Look! All these years I've been slaving for you and never disobeyed your orders. Yet you never gave me even a young goat so I could celebrate with my friends. But when this son of yours who has squandered your property with prostitutes comes home, you kill the fattened calf for him!'

"'My son,' the father said, 'you are always with me, and everything I have is yours. But we had to celebrate and be glad, because this brother of yours was dead and is alive again; he was lost and is found.'"

Luke 15:11-32

Because children typically receive their inheritance upon their father's death, it was extremely unusual for the younger son to ask for his inheritance while his father was still alive. Unfortunately, he didn't want this money for altruistic purposes. He wanted it because he was impatient to pursue a life of pleasure and flashy living. It must be remembered, though, that the younger son's selfish life choices did not change his identity.

With plenty of money to spend, the young man made lots of friends to help him spend it. However, when the money ran out, so did his so-called friends. Still, having friends and losing friends did not change his identity.

This young man sank so low that the only job he could find was tending to someone else's pigs. Even the pigs had more than he did because they had food to eat while he longed to be able to share their scraps. This also did not change his identity.

Finally, in great shame, the young man returned to his father, humbled himself, and asked to be treated as a servant rather than as his son. Even if the father were to have respected his son's request, treating his son as a servant would not have changed his identity. But the father, instead, ordered a celebration—a huge feast honoring his son. Why? Why would the father choose to honor this son who had behaved so badly?

The answer to this question is found in the father's response to the older son who was angry and hurt that his father appeared to be rewarding his younger brother's bad behavior rather than his own good behavior. The father was overjoyed to have his son back and treated him as royalty, not as a servant, because no matter what this young man had done, his true identity was that he was his father's son.

In the same way, you are a child of our Heavenly Father, and that—not your behavior—is the basis for your identity. If you are trying to find your identity in your experiences and performance, you need to change your perspective. I have developed exercises that can help you do just that. Not only do we use these exercises at our clinic, I use them myself when my sense of identity becomes skewed by my own experiences. Tim's story perfectly illustrates these exercises.

Tim Finds a New Life After Retiring From Professional Soccer

Tim, a retired professional soccer player, began to have problems in his early 40's. His wife thought he was going through a mid-life crisis. He was drinking too much and cheating on her. Tim was missing the attention he had received before his retirement. He wasn't signing as many autographs and didn't have any more endorsements. To compensate, he was constantly seeking ways to get back in the limelight.

At his first appointment with me, Tim confided that he no longer knew who he was. Without his soccer career, he believed he was "a nobody." I helped Tim understand that by building his identity on his career, when his playing days ended, his sense of identity ended too.

Tim had developed the following distorted beliefs.

1. He believed that being a celebrity added more value to his identity when, in reality, a person's value actually lies in his or her personhood.
2. He believed that his identity was determined by what people thought of him. This is false as well. Often other people do not even understand their own identities, so their opinions on someone else's identity have little true value.
3. He believed that because he was a celebrity he didn't need God. Therefore, what God had to say about anything—including his identity—had no meaning to him. Unfortunately, failure to acknowledge God is the greatest of pitfalls.
4. He believed that a person can lose his or her identity. This is also untrue. Since human beings do not choose or earn their identities, they also cannot lose them.

I helped Tim separate his true identity from his work, activities, and behaviors by taking him through the following exercises.

1. I had Tim write down all the words he could find that he associated with identity and then bring his list to a session to process them. This helped us both to identify where his distorted beliefs were lodged in his brain.
2. Next I had Tim go back in his mind to the time before he had become a soccer player, write down what he had thought about himself then, and compare that to how he felt about himself at the time of our sessions.
3. The next exercise I gave Tim was based on Genesis 1:26-27. Tim was to write out what God says about his identity based on those verses and compare his own view of his identity with God's view.
4. At this point, Tim was ready for identity affirming Scriptures. I had Tim gather a dozen Scriptures that speak to how God sees us and asked him to read through and pray those Scriptures daily.
5. For his final exercise, I asked Tim to read the life of King David and write down David's character defects. Then I asked Tim to write down God's view on David's heart.

I cannot emphasize enough the importance of a healthy identity which empowers your ability to function, perceive accurately, relate to others, and experience life as Jesus promised when He stated in John 10:10, "I have come that they may have life, and have it to the full."

Chapter 7

Managing Your Behavior

Therefore, I urge you, brothers and sisters, in view of God's mercy, to offer your bodies as a living sacrifice, holy and pleasing to God—this is your true and proper worship. Do not conform to the pattern of this world, but be transformed by the renewing of your mind. Then you will be able to test and approve what God's will is—his good, pleasing and perfect will.

Romans 12:1-2

After addressing the issue of managing your identity, managing your behavior is the next logical area of focus. Remember that your identity is not based on your behavior, your job, your status in society, your looks, or what others think about you. You and I are who God made us based on His image. However, this doesn't mean that we can behave badly. In fact, this should actually produce more responsible behaviors in us.

The new life that Jesus promises has power to change how we behave. As Paul told the Corinthians, "Therefore, if anyone is in Christ, the new creation has come: The old has gone, the new is here!" (2 Corinthians 5:17) The Corinthians faced challenges stemming from the gross immoralities of their city. Though they were new creatures in Christ, many of them struggled with the old ways of thinking, believing, and behaving. Paul was telling them that as Christians their old behaviors could be left behind through the power of Christ who lived in them.

For Christians, good behavior is based on the power of Christ working within us. We cannot take a legalistic path to holiness. This is the message I want to communicate clearly. I don't want anyone reading this chapter to think that I am talking about some behavior modification program or about human effort.

Romans 12:1 clearly states that we are only able to be transformed because of God's mercy. We are transformed through offering our bodies—which carry out the old sinful behaviors—as living sacrifices to God. In the old covenant, God was offered dead sacrifices on the altar, but a living sacrifice is a much better one.

Paul was concerned with the ways the Roman Christians were behaving, and he wanted their actions to be in accordance with their faith. He wanted them to know and agree with the perfect will of God—to live in ways pleasing to Him as their true and proper worship. He told the Romans that the transformation of their behaviors would come through the renewing of their minds.

Just like the Romans, as Christians today:

1. We need to present our bodies to God if we are going to have success in overcoming old patterns of behavior.
2. We can't do this through our own efforts. We need to be transformed.
3. We need to know the will of God.
4. We need our minds renewed.

If we want to manage our behaviors, we need to do so *God's* way. Just as we need God's mercy for salvation, we need God's mercy for everyday living because in our own strength we will fail. Our desires may lead us into bad behaviors, and since we can't tame our bodies, we need to offer them to God. It is this act of sacrificing our bodies to God that lets the power of Christ transform us through the renewing of our minds. When our minds are renewed, then we can know the perfect will of God.

The areas of the brain associated with managing behavior are the fontal cortex, the Broca's area (will), the hippocampus (mind), the olfactory area, and the brain stem (body). It's interesting to me that the body, mind, and will are the very areas Paul is isolating in Romans 12:1-2.

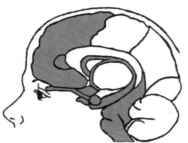

Frontal Cortex, Broca's Area, Hippocampus, Olfactory Area, Brainstem

Ordinarily, people think of the frontal cortex as the part of the brain that is most involved in purposeful behavior. This is the area of focus for behavior modification practices. However, I have discovered from my research that though behavior is lived out in the frontal areas of the brain, it is born inside the area that holds our beliefs and values: the mind. I have also discovered that the body, its cravings, and its drives are controlled by chemicals that don't listen to the mind and frontal cortex easily. Amazingly, Paul is saying pretty much the same thing in Romans 12:1-2.

When Paul says to offer our bodies as living sacrifices, he knows our bodies sometimes crave things that are sinful. The hypothalamus, the pituitary gland, and the rest of the endocrine system produce hormones and other chemicals which have a powerful impact on us. Think about how hard it is for people with addictions, anxiety, depression, or other physiological problems to use willpower to overcome such issues. They must often depend on strong medications to combat their powerful physiological reactions. No wonder Paul says to offer these areas to God.

Then Paul says we need to have our minds renewed. The parts of the brain covered in the chapter on managing our thinking are the same areas involved in managing our behaviors. Remember, our minds influence our behaviors. To review, our experiences stored as memories in the hippocampus shape our belief systems which form our value systems which govern how we behave. That's why we need our minds renewed.

Finally, Paul says that when we offer our bodies as living sacrifices holy and pleasing to God and are transformed by the renewing of our minds, then we will know the perfect will of God. In other words, if we let God direct *our* wills, it will be easy for us to know *His* will. As previously noted, I have identified the Broca's area—the control center of the frontal lobe—as the seat of the human will. Thus it is important that we strengthen this area of the brain.

Here I would like to provide you with some exercises for strengthening your will. Usually when we seek God's will, we are really seeking that which benefits us. Then we wonder why God doesn't answer our prayers. God's answer may be that our desires are not in accordance with His will. Since it's a lot easier for us to follow God and do His will when our hearts are in it, this first group of exercises will help you learn to desire God and His ways.

1. Philippians 2:13 states, "for it is God who works in you to will and to act in order to fulfill his good purpose." Consider how your life is fulfilling the purposes of God. How do the things you do line up with God's objectives for your life?
    - Write down your life objectives
    - Explain how your objectives can serve God.
2. 1 John 5:14 tells us, "This is the confidence we have in approaching God: that if we ask anything according to his will, he hears us." We all ask God for things we think we want that may not be in accordance with His will. Therefore, we need to know how to determine whether or not something we desire is the will of God.
    - Write down the things you consider to be the desires of your heart.
    - Delineate why each of your desires would be in accordance with God's desires.
3. In Psalm 40:8, David declares, "I desire to do your will, my God; your law is within my heart." David submitted his will to God because he desired God's will more than his own. Consequently, God declared David to be a man after His own heart.
    - Make a list of some things you really wanted to do that you actually got to do.

- Make a list of some things you think God would really want you to do.

The second group of exercises is designed to help you to learn how to make willful choices. You must do this in the way Peter encouraged the elect in 1 Peter 3:16-17, "keeping a clear conscience, so that those who speak maliciously against your good behavior in Christ may be ashamed of their slander. For it is better, if it is God's will, to suffer for doing good than for doing evil." These exercises help people think through the choices they make. Sometimes we shy away from making hard choices, but we all need to attempt to make good choices even when those choices are not popular.

1. The human will is not like God's will. God's will is superior. 2 Peter 1:21 says, "For prophecy never had its origin in the human will, but prophets, though human, spoke from God as they were carried along by the Holy Spirit." These prophets set aside their own wills so the Holy Spirit could speak through them to prophecy what God willed. We need to be able to distinguish our human promptings from those of the Holy Spirit.
    - We have all had times when we believed God spoke to us. Write down specific times in your life when you think this was the case for you.
    - Explain why you believe it was God you heard and not your own thoughts.
2. The human will is vulnerable to being taken captive by the enemy. As Paul wrote to Timothy, "And the Lord's servant must not be quarrelsome but must be kind to everyone, able to teach, not resentful. Opponents must be gently instructed, in the hope that God will grant them repentance leading them to a knowledge of the truth, and that they will come to their senses and escape from the trap of the devil, who has taken them captive to do his will." (2 Timothy 2:24-26) Because the devil would also like us to do his will, it is important that we recognize his attempts to entrap us.
    - We have all had times when we believed the enemy was attacking us. Write down specific times in your

life when you think you were under an attack of the enemy
- Explain why you believe what you were experiencing was an enemy attack.

3. The will is crucial when it comes to impulse control. In addressing the issue of sexual purity among single people, Paul wrote to the Corinthians, "But the man who has settled the matter in his own mind, who is under no compulsion but has control over his own will, and who has made up his mind not to marry the virgin—this man also does the right thing." (1 Corinthians 7:37) Basically, Paul was commending the willful decision to do the right thing.
- What willful decisions have you made to overcome the enemy in the area of impulse control?
- What willful decisions have you made in order to defeat the enemy specifically in the area of sexual purity?

So, the way to strengthen your will is by redirecting it to God through the Scriptures and submitting yourself to the leading of the Holy Spirit. We ask for things from God in a different manner when our wills are submitted to Him. Rather than trying to better ourselves for our own benefit, we will want to please God and advance His Kingdom.

It seems many Christians today treat God as a type of investment banker. They want Him to give them material blessings—great jobs, lots of money, and nice things—in exchange for their giving or obedience. But we should do the will of God for His glory rather than to receive His blessings. Often He blesses us anyway, but that should not be the main reason for following Him.

Let's not be like the 19th century "rice Christians" named so by missionaries in Asian countries who realized many of their converts had turned to God for material benefits like food and medical supplies. Once their socio-economic situations improved, they no longer needed "rice" and drifted away from the church. We don't want future generations to remember us as the "material blessings Christians."

Chapter 8

Managing Your Relationships

Therefore if you have any encouragement from being united with Christ, if any comfort from his love, if any common sharing in the Spirit, if any tenderness and compassion, then make my joy complete by being like-minded, having the same love, being one in spirit and one of mind. Do nothing out of selfish ambition or vain conceit. Rather, in humility value others above yourselves, not looking to your own interests but each of you to the interests of others.

In your relationships with one another, have the same mindset as Christ Jesus: Who, being in very nature God, did not consider equality with God something to be used to his own advantage; rather, he made himself nothing by taking the very nature of a servant, being made in human likeness.

Philippians 2:1-7

Philippians 2:1-7 speaks to how we should relate to others. Here Paul tells the Philippians to be tender and compassionate, to shun selfish ambition and pride, and to humbly place the interests of others above their own. He encourages them to be like Jesus who, though He is God, never used that fact to His advantage but, rather, took the very nature of a servant. How often do we handle our own relationships as Paul directs?

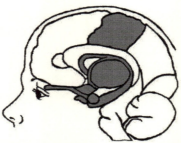

Motor and Sensory Cortex, Hippocampus, Thalamus, Olfactory Area

The areas of the brain heavily involved in relating include the mind (hippocampus), the heart (thalamus), our reactionary regions (olfactory area), and most significantly, the motor and sensory cortex. Though it is known that the motor and sensory cortex is involved in controlling muscles that move the body, I have discovered that it directs mental functions as well. All our five senses—sight, taste, smell, touch, and hearing—are used here to allow or disallow input into and out from our brains. This is what I call the relating loop.

The relating loop is formed very early in childhood development. Clearly, even babies are able to give and receive input. Without words or much purposeful body movement, they are still able to communicate with others. These interactions become the learning ground for adult ways of relating.

How we were raised has tremendous impact on our relationships. The dysfunctional relational patterns we learned in childhood often make it difficult for us to relate as Paul instructs. Following are some of the most common relational patterns that are the source of relationship discord.

1. First, let's look at control-based relating. In this pattern, people seek to control others in relationships because they believe themselves to be superior to them. They think their relationships will only work if they are the ones managing them. Often, these types of people mistake control for leadership. However, those in relationship with them feel dominated and overpowered.

People who feel the need to control others usually learned in early childhood that there was no one they could count on. They learned to be independent and only rely on themselves. They want others to be just like them—to believe and to behave as they do—and if they are not, they will push to try to change them. These people tend to handle their relationships as they would handle their businesses.

It is not uncommon for people who like to control others to get into relationships with overly dependent people who love to have others take care of them. We will look at overly dependent relating next.

2. An overly dependent interpersonal pattern is as unhealthy as an overly controlling one. The overly dependent person is passive and relates from a one-down position: considering the other person to be smarter and better in many ways and looking to him or her to be the leader and provider in the relationship. It is common for the two people to relate more as parent and child than as peers. This can lead to resentment for the more dominant person and may even lead him or her to develop an abusive attitude toward the needy one in the relationship.

People who are overly dependent were usually raised in a highly controlled, extremely critical environment. Such people often lack the confidence to run their own lives.

3. Anxiety-based relating is our third problematic relational pattern. Remember, anxiety is fear that is unfounded. People who relate from a position of anxiety are full of unnecessary worry. They do not trust others and believe that people, in general, are unsafe. It's also hard for them to trust God. Thus they put up walls or isolate to protect themselves from being hurt even though they do not have rational reasons for their fears. This makes them hard to get to know or to get close to.

Growing up in a traumatic, fear-producing environment in which a child does not feel safe produces anxiety. In addition, being raised by an unpredictable parent or parents can lead to anxiety-based relating.

4. When people relate from an emotion-based perspective, they allow too much emotion to override their reasoning. They create lots of drama, and it's draining to be in relationship with them because of the high intensity. There is no

reasoning with them, and their stability is, at best, questionable. They are overly sensitive and get their feelings hurt easily.

Usually, their emotions overwhelm them because they never learned how to control them when they were growing up. They were spoiled by their parents and allowed to let their emotions fly anywhere and anytime with no redirection. Often, one or both of their parents never learned how to manage his or her emotions.

When we have sustained emotional trauma, it becomes difficult for us to relate as the Bible tells us we should because our brains expend energy wrestling with the hurts rather than on maintaining healthy relationships. It is vital for us to address these hurts before we can practice healthy relational skills. Though there are some excellent seminars, books, and videos available on relationships, it is my opinion that if they don't emphasize the importance of addressing past hurts and understanding how they impact our current situations, they will be ineffective. All the best skills in the world, all the best books on communication, lovemaking, etc., will not help if there are deeper hurts and negative beliefs impacting relational patterns.[4]

I often hear people claim they will not repeat the parenting mistakes their parents made only to find they are, indeed, following in their parents' footsteps. I also hear people say their next relationship will be different from their previous ones only to find themselves in the same relationship dilemmas. Why? Because they never corrected the root cause of their relationship problems.

---

[4] *Marriage Today*, with Jimmy and Karen Evans, is a TV show as well as a ministry dedicated to helping people keep marriages and families together. Jimmy and Karen understand the impact of past hurts on our relationships. I personally went through their marriage video series. Wonderful stuff. They also have books that I highly recommend.

Though I don't do it as much now, I used to do a lot of marriage counseling. I can't tell you how many times I would hear a couple say that they needed a fresh start. By this they usually meant they wanted to be in new relationships with different people. But, unfortunately, when they got into new relationships, the same problems popped up. When they would come back to see me about this phenomenon, I would tell them that even though they were with new people, their old selves were still with them causing the same problems they had experienced in their past relationships. Most of us want to look at the other person's problems rather than our own.

When I was around 19 years of age, I heard a teacher say that rather than focusing on finding Miss or Mr. Right, we should focus on *being* Miss or Mr. Right. This is excellent advice not only for marriages but other relationships as well. Many people seek good, quality friendships. They want to be in relationships with people in whom they can trust and rely, but they don't give a thought to whether they are trustworthy and reliable themselves.

I find so often that people don't really understand how relationships work. As Philippians 2:5-7 says, we should have the same mindset as Christ, taking the very nature of a servant in our relationships with others. How can you apply this principle in your own relationships?

There are some practical things you can do to manage your relational patterns, but first you need to learn how to manage your mindset. The mind (hippocampus) is the source of what we believe and the values we hold. Therefore, when Paul says we are to have the same mindset as Christ, he means our beliefs and values concerning relationships should be grounded in the teachings of Christ. That can only happen when we feed our minds with Scriptures and teachings that support Christ's views on the subject. Because the mind influences how the rest of the brain processes information, what we believe will eventually show up in how we behave. Our behaviors, in turn, affect our relationships. Therefore, to change how we relate, we need to change our beliefs and value systems. There are four major belief systems with their accompanying values that influence how we relate.

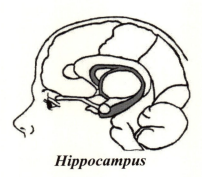

Hippocampus

1. *I am a "bad" person who shouldn't be in a relationship.* This belief is usually the result of emotional pain from traumatic childhood experiences. Children who suffer a great deal of physical and/or verbal abuse or neglect may conclude that they are bad or even evil and may form negative opinions of others as well. They may come to believe that people are nothing but a source of pain.

    Unfortunately, those with this viewpoint often engage in behaviors that reinforce their beliefs and value systems. They may exhibit bad behavior patterns and even get in trouble with the law. They may repeatedly hurt people, and in turn, people may not like them. Typically, they relate out of anger, lashing out at others and antagonizing them or creating thick walls of self-protection. Their explosive, angry outbursts cause people to fear them. This leads to isolation.

    People in these situations need to get to the root cause of their beliefs and ascertain the reasons for their anger. Usually they engage in this type of anger to cover up and protect themselves from deep hurt. Because they were not valued by their abusers, they place a poor value on others. They need to go through an inner healing process and then be educated in healthy relational patterns.

2. *I can only trust and rely on myself.* People who hold this belief determined early in life that they couldn't count on anyone, so they learned to depend on themselves and retained this self-sufficiency into adulthood. For people with this mindset, no one can quite live up to their standards. Because

they can't allow themselves to turn to anyone else, they panic if they themselves get something wrong.

These people are often so self-sufficient that they have a hard time trusting God. The idea of grace is difficult for them to accept. They also have a hard time with love and affection. They are prone to legalism and value the Law because rules and structure give them guidance.

Because they value performance, productive people are more estimable in their eyes. They believe that "God helps those who help themselves," and they usually accomplish a great deal in life in areas like business that require drive, ambition, and self-will. Unfortunately, however, they struggle in relationships because relationships cannot be run like a business.

People who are overly self-reliant carry hurts of abandonment and neglect which they may mask by justifying the pain they experienced. They often make excuses for those who hurt them, defending them as having done the best they could. But what they really need to do is admit they are hurt and express the appropriate feelings. This is hard for them to do because they think it is wrong and dishonoring to their parents and others who were their superiors. They also need to learn to enter into God's rest because they are likely to experience burnout due to their tendency toward workaholism. They need to learn to accept God's grace.[5]

3. *I am so special that things should revolve around me. I deserve the very best.* We are each special to God in different ways, but this belief takes that knowledge to a self-centered level. We are not more special than His other children, and everything does not revolve around us. So many Christians believe that they deserve the best, but this is not true. We get what we do by the grace of God. Remember, Jesus said in Matthew 19:30, "But many who are first will be last, and

---

[5] If you are one of these types of people, I highly recommend Joseph Prince's teachings on grace. This will help change your mindset and improve your relationships.

many who are last will be first," and again in Matthew 20:16, "So the last will be first and the first will be last."

A few years ago, I went to the DMV office to get my driver's license renewed. Like the others there, I had to take a number and wait until it was called. A well-dressed lady in her 30's kept pacing up and down, obviously in a hurry. Finally, she approached an older woman with a number that was lower than hers and asked her if she would be willing to trade numbers. I wasn't far from where they were standing and overheard her say, "Ma'am, praise God, I need to get my license renewed and get back to work. May I have your number and you have mine? Halleluiah!" I was stunned and so was the woman, who answered, "I am sorry, Ma'am, but you need to wait your turn."

Next the young lady looked right at me, smiled a huge smile, and asked me if I was the kind of gentleman who would give his seat to a lady. I said I was—not just to a lady but to anyone in need. So she gave me her song and dance about being a daughter of the King, etc. When she finished, I told her that I was glad she was a daughter of the King, but He has many sons and daughters—including both the lady she had first approached and me. I then asked her why she thought she was more important than the rest of His family. For a moment, she just stood there, shocked.

Changing the subject, she asked me where I went to church, and I told her. I asked her where she went to church, and she not only told me where but gushed about how it was the biggest and best. I told her I knew her church well and was good friends with the pastors there. I mentioned the names of my friends on the pastoral staff, and she had wonderful things to say about them. Then I asked her if her attitude would be considered acceptable at her church. She didn't have an answer.

This is an example of the self-centeredness that can result when people feel insecure and seek for ways to mitigate those feelings. These types of people demand a great deal of attention and have a hard time if that attention goes elsewhere. Unfortunately, others don't want to be around, let alone in a relationship with, self-centered people.

Self-centeredness is common among people who received too much attention and were spoiled in childhood. They were kids who got everything they asked for and more. They received no discipline, and they grew up with no sense of others. Their parents thought they were loving their kids, but they were actually crippling them for the future.

4. *Happiness can be found in material things, and life should be full of fun.* Certainly, we all want to be happy and to have fun in life. But many of us need a better understanding of happiness and fun. First of all, there is no correlation between happiness and material things. Since material things can be lost, it is dangerous for us to try to base our happiness on our possessions because then our happiness can be lost with the loss of those possessions. Materialism has been proven to build superficial people, not solid societies.

There is also a problem with the mindset that focuses on enjoyment of life experiences. There is nothing wrong with having fun and enjoying life, but there is a real problem with making life all about fun and pleasure. There are many experiences in life that require us to be serious and sober. Solomon, with his great wisdom from God, expressed in Ecclesiastes 3:1, "There is a time for everything and a season for every activity under the heavens." He went on to say in Ecclesiastes 3:4 that there is a time for us to weep and a time for us to laugh, a time for us to mourn and a time for us to dance.

Life is about balance, and people with this mindset do not have a good balance in their lives. Those in relationship with people whose lives are out of balance in this way have to cater to their overblown desires for fun and pleasure or deal with their frustrations and complaints. This mindset keeps people from growing in maturity; therefore, when dealing with people with this perspective, we work on helping them to mature mentally, emotionally, and in some cases, spiritually.

When it comes to managing relationships, it's important to be able to recognize unhealthy relational patterns and the mindsets that produce them and to heal whatever is at the heart of them. We also need to submit ourselves to the teaching of Scripture, especially Philippians 2:5, in how we relate to one another.

Chapter 9

Managing Your Spiritual Life

> Therefore, my dear friends, as you have always obeyed—not only in my presence, but now much more in my absence—continue to work out your salvation with fear and trembling, for it is God who works in you to will and to act in order to fulfill his good purpose.
>
> Do everything without grumbling or arguing, so that you may become blameless and pure, "children of God without fault in a warped and crooked generation." Then you will shine among them like stars in the sky as you hold firmly to the word of life.
>
> Philippians 2:12-16

Many books have been written on the disciplines of the spiritual life such as prayer, Bible study, witnessing, and discipleship, among others. I will not be addressing these specific disciplines here but will, instead, be focusing on how to manage the regions of the brain that represent the soul, the heart, the mind, the emotions, and that handle inner vision and perception. These are the areas that I have discovered carry out key roles in our spiritual lives.

To manage our lives, we must manage our brains, and this is true of the spiritual aspects of our lives as well as the others. Many Christians are under the impression that our brains run the academic, physical, mental, and even emotional facets of our lives but are excluded when it comes to spiritual matters. In this chapter, I want to emphasize that our spiritual lives are managed through our brains and show you how you can use this knowledge to have a better experience in your Christian walk.

First, let's look at the nature of man. What is man? Where did he come from? What is he made of?

When I was in college, my biology professor said something I have not forgotten. He told us that if we were to construct a human being from scratch, the body (which God made out of the dust of the earth) would be the cheapest and easiest part to make. He said it would cost us less than a dollar—$.98 to be exact. The real cost and challenge, he said, would be to make what controls the body—the brain—because human beings cannot build a big enough or efficient enough computer to do what the human brain does. I remember thinking how much time, effort, and money we put into the upkeep of our bodies while often neglecting the upkeep of our all-important brains.

Genesis 2:7 says, "Then the LORD God formed a man from the dust of the ground and breathed into his nostrils the breath of life, and the man became a living being." It's that breath of life from God that made us living, breathing creatures. Otherwise, we would have remained just dust. The King James Version of this Scripture passage says that "man became a living soul." Clearly, the body gets its life from the soul, the soul gets its life from the spirit, and the spirit gets its life from God.

God made man in His image and breathed life into him. He did not do this with any other of His creations. Out of all He created, man was, and is, unique. We are spiritually based creatures who need God to sustain our existence. Without a doubt, the understanding of how to manage the spiritual aspects of our lives is one of the most important.

So how do you go about managing your spiritual nature? When Adam and Eve sinned, mankind's spiritual nature died. Thus, your spiritual nature must be made alive again through salvation in Jesus Christ. If you are not a believer, performing all sorts of good spiritual exercises will not awaken your spiritual nature. You must come to know Jesus as your Lord and Savior. This is exactly what Paul expressed to the Ephesians.

> As for you, you were dead in your transgressions and sins, in which you used to live when you followed the ways of this world and of the ruler of the kingdom of the air, the spirit who is now at work in those who are disobedient. All of us also lived among them at one time, gratifying the cravings of our flesh and following its desires and thoughts. Like the rest, we were by nature deserving of wrath. But because of his

great love for us, God, who is rich in mercy, made us alive with Christ even when we were dead in transgressions—it is by grace you have been saved.

Ephesians 2:1-5

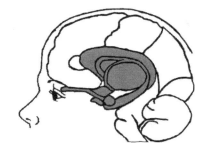

Corpus Callosum, Hippocampus, Basal Ganglia, Thalamus, Olfactory Area

As you can see from this passage, we need to manage our spiritual lives or our old natures, driven by cravings of the flesh and by the power of the ruler of the kingdom of the air, will take over and adversely affect our spiritual experiences. To that end, let's look at the areas of the brain that most significantly impact spirituality— the corpus callosum, the hippocampus (mind), the basal ganglia, the thalamus (heart), and the olfactory area (soul). We'll begin with the heart.

It's clear the importance Scripture places on the heart. In fact, the very first commandment concerns the heart. In Matthew 22:34-38, Jesus tells a Pharisee that "the first and greatest commandment" is, "Love the Lord your God with all your heart and with all your soul and with all your mind." When God speaks to Samuel about choosing a king in 1 Samuel 16:7, He declares, "The LORD does not look at the things people look at. People look at the outward appearance, but the LORD looks at the heart." In Psalm 51:10, David cries out to the Lord, "Create in me a pure heart, O God." In verse 17 he continues, "My sacrifice, O God, is a broken spirit; a broken and contrite heart you, God, will not despise." Jesus, addressing the Pharisees in Matthew 12:34, says, "For the mouth speaks what the heart is full of." And in Ephesians 3:17, Paul prays that Christ may dwell in the hearts of the Ephesian Christians through faith.

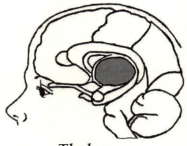

Thalamus

I have found through my research that when a person's heart area of the brain (thalamus) contains faith, he or she treasures the things of God deeply, even if it may not show on the outside. Authentic faith has to start with the heart.

The thalamus receives all incoming information from the outside and distributes it to the rest of the brain. Therefore, it's not surprising that Jesus said, "The mouth speaks what the heart is full of." (Luke 6:45) I have also discovered that people with unhealed wounds and memories of abuse and trauma tend to bury them here. In addition, Jeremiah 17:9 warns, "The heart is deceitful above all things and beyond cure. Who can understand it?" Thus it is clear that if we want to manage our spiritual lives, we must begin by managing what's in our hearts. If we have unhealed wounds, deceit, and other unpleasant things in our hearts, we must deal with them, or they will poison our lives.

The second important area in managing our spiritual lives is the mind (hippocampus). We need to operate with the mind of Christ, and as we learned from Romans 12:2, we need our minds renewed so that we will not be conformed to this world.

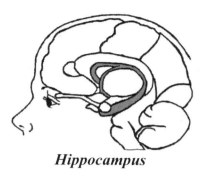

Hippocampus

David asked the Lord to examine his heart and mind because he understood their importance to God. (Psalm 26:2) Concerning the greatest commandment, Jesus said again in Mark 12:30, "Love the Lord your God with all your heart and with all your soul and with all your mind and with all your strength." Paul told the Romans, "The mind governed by the flesh is death, but the mind governed by the Spirit is life and peace. The mind governed by the flesh is hostile to God; it does not submit to God's law, nor can it do so. Those who are in the realm of the flesh cannot please God." (Romans 8:6-8) Peter warned concerning the end times, "The end of all things is near. Therefore be alert and of sober mind so that you may pray." (I Peter 4:7)

The bottom line is that we need our minds leading us, not opposing us, in the process of managing our spiritual lives. This is why Paul told the Corinthians, "We demolish arguments and every pretension that sets itself up against the knowledge of God, and we take captive every thought to make it obedient to Christ." (2 Corinthians 10:5) One of the best ways to do this is to fill our minds with the Word of God so that our thinking processes and belief systems are influenced by God's Word. Remember, Hebrews 4:12 says, "For the word of God is alive and active. Sharper than any double-edged sword, it penetrates even to dividing soul and spirit, joints and marrow; it judges the thoughts and attitudes of the heart."

In Acts 17:11, we read about the Berean Jewish believers who "examined the Scriptures every day to see if what Paul said was true." Studying the Bible is one of the disciplines of the early church that the modern day church doesn't practice much. The average believer today knows very little about the Bible. In fact, many of the false religions in the world currently spend more time and effort understanding and teaching their false word than the modern day church does understanding and teaching the Bible. The importance of studying the Scriptures can't be overstated because when the Word of God occupies the mind, it is able to give direction to the entire brain.

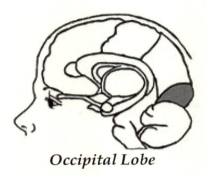

Occipital Lobe

The third area of the brain I found to be crucial in managing our spiritual lives is the visual cortex of the right hemisphere in the occipital lobe. We know that our left visual cortex, our seeing brain, processes our vision. Through my research, I have discovered that it is the right visual cortex that gives us our inner vision. This is the brain's ability to forecast into the future with hope, anticipation, motivation, and the drive to succeed. It is the part of the brain that exercises faith—a crucial aspect of our relationship with God. We come to God by faith, and we became His children by placing our faith in the saving work of His Son, Jesus Christ.

Hebrews 11 is known as the faith chapter in the Bible. In the first verse, faith is defined as "confidence in what we hope for and assurance about what we do not see." In the sixth verse, Paul writes, "And without faith it is impossible to please God, because anyone who comes to him must believe that he exists and that he rewards those who earnestly seek him." In the rest of Hebrews 11, Paul gives examples of people who practiced faith: "the ancients" who "were commended for their faith." (Hebrews 11:2)

The ability to have this type of faith depends greatly on how well the visual cortex is functioning. I have treated people with very serious psychological problems in other regions of their brains, but faith in the area of the visual cortex made them able to push through the obstacles they faced. Why is faith so important in this area? Certainly, faith is important in the mind and in the heart, but faith in the visual cortex is even more crucial because that is the area of the brain that provides us with our overall outlook on life.

So how can you strengthen your visual cortex so that your faith guides your outlook on life? Following are the steps we recommend at our clinic to people struggling with faith issues and having difficulty trusting God.

1. When you encounter difficult times, turn to the Lord and His Word instead of focusing on your unfortunate state of affairs.
2. Practice looking at your situation through the eyes of God. Try to see things the way God sees them rather than the way you do.
3. Go to Hebrews 11 and see if you can find an example of someone whose circumstances closely resemble yours. Look at how the situation was handled and apply what he or she did to your situation.
4. Find a trusted, believing friend or pastor to pray with you over your circumstances.
5. Make a habit of reading books on faith and biographies of people who lived by faith.
6. Reflect back on your life journey to those times when God came through for you and then thank Him for doing so.
7. Make sure an attack from the enemy is not causing your circumstances. If you do determine that it is, resist the devil so he will flee from you. How do you do that? Here are some practical ways to resist the enemy's attacks.

    • The enemy always has reasons for attacking you. To resist him, you need to find out what those reasons are.
    • Discover the stronghold or legal ground the devil is using as justification for his attack.

- Determine if there is any kind of benefit you are receiving by keeping the struggle going.
- Reject and renounce all areas that have given the enemy an inroad and refuse to allow them in your life again.

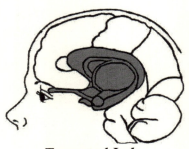

Temporal Lobe

The soul is the final section of the brain that is important in managing our spiritual lives. When Paul expresses in Ephesians 3:16, "I pray that out of his glorious riches he may strengthen you with power through his Spirit in your inner being," he is praying for the Ephesians' souls. I have identified the inner being in the brain as the limbic system in the temporal lobe. This is the area of the brain where the heart, mind, emotions, and desires reside.

Since I have already covered the heart and mind, I now want to focus on emotions and desires (the corpus callosum, basal ganglia, and olfactory area) which play a very important part in managing our spiritual lives.

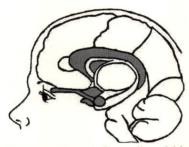

Corpus Callosum, Basal Ganglia, Olfactory Area

I once conducted a study on spiritual disciplines that focused on the impact of faith on evangelical believers as compared to charismatic believers. I found evangelical believers to be strong in the areas of knowledge of the Word and principles of faith. They were good at teaching Scripture, recognizing error, and presenting truth when confronted with false teachings. On the other hand, they were weak in the areas of the emotional experience and outward demonstration of their faith. Evangelicals seem to experience their Christianity in an almost private way, benefitting them internally only with very little outward value to the other believers around them.

Conversely, their charismatic brothers and sisters were strong in the areas of their experience and outward expression of their faith and in their love of other believers. But their faith tended to go up and down with their emotions, and their heavy reliance on emotions, at times, undermined their ability to think doctrinally and to recognize false teachings when they were presented to them. Some built doctrines out of their experiences instead of letting doctrine guide their experiences.

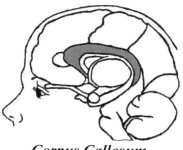

Corpus Callosum

This study confirmed that emotions are necessary for believers to fully experience their spiritual lives, but their emotions need to be balanced with strong knowledge of the Word and of principles of faith. The more areas of the brain that are engaging spiritually, the better a person is able to manage his or her spiritual life.

The corpus callosum not only connects the two hemispheres of the brain but, I have learned, connects emotions to the entire brain—much as the internet connects our world today. Thus I can't emphasize enough how important it is for this area to be influenced by positive, Godly feelings. When the corpus callosum is influenced by negative emotions such as, fear, anxiety, depression, anger and hopelessness, the entire brain is deleteriously affected.

Throughout this book, I have emphasized the need for healing any unhealed wounds. Wounds can also affect how we manage our spiritual lives, especially when the traumatic experiences occupy the corpus callosum. We need the word of God, not our unhealed wounds, influencing our emotions.

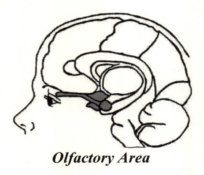

Olfactory Area

The olfactory area is not only responsible for the way we react to external perceived threats, it also impacts our desires. As it tries to regulate our reactions and appetites, all our five senses and powerful chemicals and hormones come into play. This is a very active area of the brain and has tremendous impact on our spiritual lives.

It should be common knowledge among Christians that to fully manage temptation we need to be able to manage our desires. Remember what happened to Adam and Eve in the Garden? In Genesis 2:15-17, we read that God told them not to eat of the tree of knowledge of good and evil. But in Genesis 3:1-24, we learn of their disobedience resulting in the tragic fall of man that affects all of us today. And it all started in the olfactory area of Eve's brain. Genesis 3:6 tells us, "When the woman saw that the fruit of the tree was good for food and pleasing to the eye, and also desirable for gaining wisdom, she took some and ate it." Eve failed to manage this area of her brain, and look what happened.

The Apostle John reminds us that we need to be wary of the very same temptations Eve faced.

> Do not love the world or anything in the world. If anyone loves the world, love for the Father is not in them. For everything in the world—the lust of the flesh, the lust of the eyes, and the pride of life—comes not from the Father but from the world. The world and its desires pass away, but whoever does the will of God lives forever.
>
> 1 John 2:15-17

None of us can be quick to point a finger at Adam and Eve on this issue. With so many things in the world today that flood our brains and feed our flesh, we can understand firsthand how challenging managing this area of the brain can be. However, though there can be problems in this part of the brain, I want to stress that God created the olfactory area to help us and that when it is managed well it can produce victory for us over the very issues that confronted Eve.

So how do you make sure your olfactory area influences your spiritual life positively rather than negatively? In a previous chapter, I presented ways to manage reactions and emotions. My recommendations covered this section of the brain. If you practiced managing it as I suggested, it will be a lot easier for you to apply those principles to managing your spiritual life.

As you can see from his prayer for the Ephesians below, Paul clearly understood that the soul area of the brain plays the most critical role in Christians' spiritual lives. To manage your spiritual life, you must manage your soul, and your soul must be managed by God through the Holy Spirit.

A Prayer for the Ephesians

For this reason I kneel before the Father, from whom every family in heaven and on earth derives its name. I pray that out of his glorious riches he may strengthen you with power through his Spirit in your inner being, so that Christ may dwell in your hearts through faith. And I pray that you, being rooted and established in love, may have power, together with all the Lord's holy people, to grasp how wide and long and high and deep is the love of Christ, and to know this love that surpasses knowledge—that you may be filled to the measure of all the fullness of God.

Now to him who is able to do immeasurably more than all we ask or imagine, according to his power that is at work within us, to him be glory in the church and in Christ Jesus throughout all generations, for ever and ever! Amen.

Ephesians 3:14-21

Chapter 10

Managing Your Spiritual Battles

Finally, be strong in the Lord and in his mighty power. Put on the full armor of God, so that you can take your stand against the devil's schemes. For our struggle is not against flesh and blood, but against the rulers, against the authorities, against the powers of this dark world and against the spiritual forces of evil in the heavenly realms. Therefore put on the full armor of God, so that when the day of evil comes, you may be able to stand your ground, and after you have done everything, to stand.

Ephesians 6:10-13

It may come as a shock to you to learn that you are in a war just as active as any war in the natural world. However, this conflict isn't a natural battle; it is a spiritual battle. In conventional warfare, only trained soldiers fight, and they follow rules that govern how the war is fought and that show kindness and mercy for their enemies.[6] But in this war, our enemies are spiritual beings who do not follow any rules and do not care what happens to us.

---

[6] It must be noted that there are terrorist groups today that do not follow the dictates of conventional warfare and do not deal with their enemies mercifully.

I have heard it said by many Bible teachers that if we were only allowed to have access to one book of the Bible, that book should be Ephesians. In the six chapters of Ephesians, Paul covers all the major doctrines of the faith needed to sustain our spiritual lives. The final topic he covers concerns spiritual warfare.

In chapter 1 of Ephesians, Paul addresses what theologians call predestination: namely, that God's sovereignty allows Him to pre-determine what will happen.

> For he chose us in him before the creation of the world to be holy and blameless in his sight. In love he predestined us for adoption to sonship through Jesus Christ, in accordance with his pleasure and will to the praise of his glorious grace, which he has freely given us in the One he loves.
>
> Ephesians 1:4-6

This is a very important doctrine, for it shows God's love for us. We were not an afterthought. He had us in mind before the foundation of the world.

In chapter 2, Paul teaches that salvation is by grace and not by works. Though we were dead in our transgressions and sins, "because of his great love for us, God, who is rich in mercy, made us alive with Christ." (Ephesians 2:4-5) Paul emphasizes, "For it is by grace you have been saved, through faith—and this is not from yourselves, it is the gift of God— not by works, so that no one can boast." (Ephesians 2:8-9) Salvation by grace is a crucial Christian doctrine.

In Chapter 3, Paul relays "God's marvelous plan for the Gentiles" and his insight into "the mystery of Christ." "This mystery is that through the gospel the Gentiles are heirs together with Israel, members together of one body, and sharers together in the promise in Christ Jesus." (Ephesians 3:6) The Gentiles in Paul's day understood how special this was. We are also Gentiles, and the knowledge that we are heirs together with Israel should be very special to us as well.

In chapter 4, Paul encourages Christians to live lives worthy of their calling—not to be tossed about by every wave and wind of teaching but to, instead, grow in maturity in the faith, in knowledge of the Son of God, and in the fullness of Christ. Paul emphasizes the importance of unity in the body of Christ.

> Be completely humble and gentle; be patient, bearing with one another in love. Make every effort to keep the unity of the Spirit through the bond of peace. There is one body and one Spirit, just as you were called to one hope when you were called; [5] one Lord, one faith, one baptism; one God and Father of all, who is over all and through all and in all.
>
> Ephesians 4:2-6

In the rest of the chapter, Paul gives instructions for Christian living, enumerating those things Christians should and should not do.

In Chapter 5, Paul covers the way Christians should live their married lives. He likens the relationship between husband and wife to the relationship between Christ and the church.

In Chapter 6, Paul continues to instruct Christians in the ways they should conduct themselves in their relationships and in their social lives. First he covers the parent/child relationship followed by the relationship between a master and slave (which would apply to an employer/employee relationship today). In verses 10-20 Paul concludes by relating how the Ephesian Christians could successfully practice and experience all that was theirs in Christ. This section is most often referred to as the spiritual warfare passage. Here Paul conveys 4 spiritual truths that make up the doctrine of spiritual warfare. These 4 truths are:

1. As Christians, we are already in a battle, and we'd better know how to fight by putting on the full armor of God so that we can take a stand against the devil's schemes. (Ephesians 6:11)
2. Our battle is not with "flesh and blood" but with "spiritual forces of evil." (Ephesians 6:12)
3. It takes spiritual means to fight evil. We need the armor of God to be able to stand our ground when evil comes. (Ephesians 6:13)
4. Spiritual war takes strategy just as conventional war does. So Paul uses the armor and weaponry of the Roman soldier to help Christians understand the nature of the battle against evil spiritual forces and teach them how they can be victorious. (Ephesians 6:13-18)

It's sad that so many Christians do not realize the truth that we battle principalities, powers, and evil forces—not flesh and blood. Unfortunately, Ephesians 6:10-20 is often not even taught in our churches, and I have heard some very interesting reasons why that's the case.

One explanation is that teaching or preaching on spiritual warfare would potentially scare people. The problem with this view is that fear of dealing with the enemy becomes a stronghold drawing the believer further into bondage.

Some say teaching or preaching on spiritual warfare gives more power to the enemy. There are lots of problems with this viewpoint. The biggest problem is that, according to 2 Timothy 3:16, "all scripture is God breathed and is useful for teaching, rebuking, correcting and training in righteousness." Certainly that includes the Scriptures that mention spiritual forces. Another problem with this view is that we are to "handle the word of truth correctly," (2 Timothy 2:15) and leaving out specific Scriptures for any reason is not doing so.

These reasons people give for avoiding the topic of spiritual warfare are, in my opinion, the result of spiritual warfare itself. If the truth about how to fight the enemy isn't taught, it just helps the enemy to win. The following information will help you understand the armor of God and how to apply it.

The Armor of God

Stand firm then, with the belt of truth buckled around your waist, with the breastplate of righteousness in place, and with your feet fitted with the readiness that comes from the gospel of peace. In addition to all this, take up the shield of faith, with which you can extinguish all the flaming arrows of the evil one. Take the helmet of salvation and the sword of the Spirit, which is the word of God.

And pray in the Spirit on all occasions with all kinds of prayers and requests. With this in mind, be alert and always keep on praying for all the Lord's people.

Ephesians 6:13-18

Through my years of study of both Scripture and the brain, I have seen how the human brain responds to Scripture and how certain parts of the brain work to support a life of faith. I have also seen the problems that can arise when we aren't vigilant to protect our brains from the enemy's attacks. When we truly understand how magnificently our brains were designed and all they do to sustain our lives in every dimension, the importance of protecting them becomes clear. In my opinion, the armor of God is necessary for all Christians who want their brains to work to their greatest potential. So, let's look at the armor of God from a brain perspective.

Hippocampus

The Belt of Truth

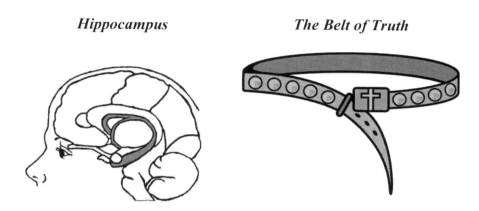

Truth in the context of this Scripture is absolute truth, which is objective and authoritative. In the brain, we find truth in the hippocampus (mind) where we receive objective guidance. Lies, trauma, pain, fear, anger, or other emotional distress in this area of the brain is an unmistakable indication that our truth armor isn't working. When inner healing and deliverance ministers speak of lies that keep people in bondage, they are referring to lies overriding truth in the hippocampus. These lies influence the frontal cortex leading people to act or live according to them rather than the truth. We cannot change our feelings or behaviors if the truth isn't established in the hippocampus. I believe this is why the belt of truth is the first part of the armor Paul mentions.

2 Timothy 1:7 says, "For God has not given us a spirit of fear; but of power, of love, and of a sound mind."[7] Though God said He gave us the spirit of a sound mind (hippocampus), I have treated many Christians whose minds were not sound. Through a process that includes applying the Word to the hippocampus, truth overcomes problems in this area of the brain.

Thalamus   ***The Breastplate of Righteousness***

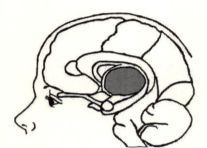

The breastplate protected the heart of the Roman soldier. Paul talks about protecting our hearts from the enemy's attacks by putting on righteousness. Much of the unrighteousness we see is the result of things like hurt, pain, anger, and hatred inhabiting the heart: the thalamus in the brain. The only righteousness we have for protection is the righteousness we receive from Christ in exchange for our sins. Self-righteousness will not protect us. On the contrary, self-righteousness leaves us wide open to defeat by the enemy.

---

[7] From the King James Version (KJV) of the Holy Bible

The Sandals of the Gospel of Peace

Motor and Sensory Cortex   *The Sandals of the Gospel of Peace*

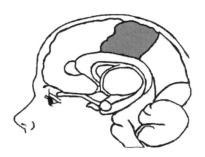

The Roman soldier wore footgear to provide good movement in battle. Paul says Christians need to be ready to move with the gospel of peace as our footgear. When Christians have the gospel of peace, it is reflected in the motor and sensory cortex which influences how we relate to the outside world and to those around us. This is especially evident with full-time Christian ministers. Though the enemy's goal is to destroy the gospel of peace, Paul reminds us that we are called to share it, which frustrates the enemy's schemes.

The Shield of Faith

Occipital Lobe   *The Shield of Faith*

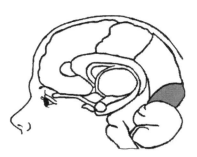

Remember, faith is defined in Hebrews 11:1 as "confidence in what we hope for and assurance about what we do not see." We also read in Hebrews 11:6, "Without faith it is impossible to please God because anyone who comes to him must believe that he exists." In our brains, faith is found in the visual cortex in the occipital lobe.

For a Roman soldier, the shield was the only active defensive weapon he had. He would strategically place it between himself and the darts coming at him, and this would not only protect him but allow him to advance forward. For us today, when we think of faith we think about getting out of some sort of trouble. But faith is meant to be active giving us the ability to advance toward the enemy. Faith in the visual cortex makes a Christian warrior tough to beat!

I have treated countless Christians who were down and had all but given up because things weren't working out for them. Because life was hard, they didn't believe in the goodness of God. Usually these Christians were having trouble in their occipital lobes. But when their occipital lobes were full of faith, nothing could stop them! They were able to agree with the Apostle Paul's great faith statement below.

> For I am convinced that neither death nor life, neither angels nor demons, neither the present nor the future, nor any powers, neither height nor depth, nor anything else in all creation, will be able to separate us from the love of God that is in Christ Jesus our Lord.
>
> (Romans 3:8)

The Helmet of Salvation

Broca's Area

The Helmet of Salvation

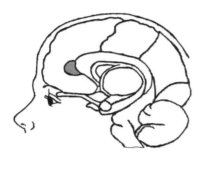

A head injury would leave a soldier unable to go on fighting. Even if it didn't render him unconscious or prove fatal, he would still be unlikely to continue. In situations of extreme stress leading to paralyzing fear, a lack of activation in the Broca's area can render a person unable to move or speak.

This small area in the brain is often referred to as "the mind's eye." In my research, I've found the Broca's area assures us of our functionality and overall safety from internal threats by searching for anything detrimental in the rest of the brain and pushing what it finds back into the cerebellum. On the flip side, since the Broca's area seems to control the whole front part of the brain, trouble here can undermine functioning and hinder anything positive happening in the frontal lobe.

It's interesting that ministers and other solid believers I have evaluated are strong in their Broca's areas. This is especially important when it comes to a believer's assurance of salvation. It's my opinion that you can be saved but unsure of your salvation, and that doubt can give the enemy an edge. I find that when believers are confident of their salvation, their faith is reflected in their Broca's areas.

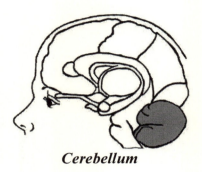

Cerebellum

The Sword of the Spirit

Basal Ganglia   *The Sword of the Spirit*

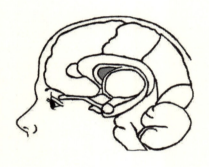   

The Holy Spirit uses the sword to "penetrate even to dividing soul, and spirit, joints and marrow; it judges the thoughts and attitudes of the heart." (Hebrews 4:12) Through neurotransmitters, the basal ganglia, which comprise the center of the brain's communication system, get messages to and influence all areas of the brain. This area also connects our psychological life to our physiological life by way of its attachment to the brainstem. Having the Word of God in the basal ganglia is the best way to defeat the enemy. He strongly desires to control this area because it gives him access to the rest of the brain.

Prayer

Olfactory Area

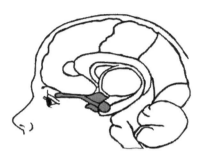 

Prayer is talking to God: letting Him know what we're feeling, thinking, and experiencing as well as acknowledging who He is and expressing our reliance on Him. In our brains, the area that drives us to pray is the olfactory area (the olfactory bulb, the hypothalamus, the amygdala, and the pituitary gland). For spiritual purposes, I call the olfactory area the SOS—save our souls—section of the brain. Fears, addictions of all kinds, overreactions to painful memories, hormonal issues, and our intuitions are all located in this area, and when we're not praying, we can be easily overcome by problems here.

But in spiritual warfare, prayer isn't just for us. When others have problems in this area of the brain, they need our prayers as well. Prayer is one way we can fight on behalf of our fellow soldiers in Christ.

I trust you see the impact your brain has on every area of your life and the importance of using the armor of God to defend it from attacks of the enemy. Protecting your brain will not only allow you to function at the highest possible level, it will also allow you to be able to commune with God as He created you to do.

Epilogue

In this book, I have outlined ways to manage your life when dealing with the most common emotional and psychological problems using a basic understanding of the brain and your faith in God and the Scriptures. I pray you have found this book helpful as you work towards healing. My hope is that the church at large might begin to appreciate the myriad tools God has given us for our complete health and learn to use them.

Historically, the church frowned upon psychiatry and psychologically based counseling. It espoused the belief that God and the church could provide all the believer needed for his or her mental health. Today the church, by and large, has come to understand the error in this thinking and has begun to utilize professionals in the mental health field—especially those professionals who share the Christian faith. As a Christian therapist, I receive many referrals from churches, and though this is a very positive development, there is still work to be done in the areas I've listed here.

1. Even now, there are churches in existence that hold with the belief that a person who has faith should not struggle with mental health issues. This thinking hurts many Christians who have a close walk with God yet grapple with mental health problems. The Bible shows clearly that Moses had anger issues. It also records a time when the Prophet Elijah was depressed and wished to die. In addition, the Bible tells us that Pastor Timothy had problems with anxiety. And the list goes on. But you can't tell me that these great men didn't have enough faith! Those who are able need to continue to educate the church on the reality of mental health concerns in the Christian community.

2. Another issue along the same lines is the notion that it is a sign of weakness to take medications. I have seen people with this perspective suffer needlessly, but when they finally began taking the right medications, they were able to feel and

function so much better. Let me clarify that I am not pushing medications, but there are certain situations in which the smartest thing for a person to do is to take an appropriate prescription.

3. Another mistaken concept in the church today is that there's no reason to remember past trauma and work it through because it's all "under the blood." This is a misunderstanding about the meaning of the phrase because "under the blood" is a positional truth which still leaves us with a responsibility to work out our own salvation with fear and trembling. In the eyes of God, all our sins are forgiven and we are justified, but we still live in earthen vessels and will continue to have problems we must face and work through with God's help.

4. There are those who believe that healing of the soul or the mind should be instantaneous, as we sometimes see with physical healings. Of course there is no reason why God can't instantaneously heal emotional and psychological problems, but to declare that this should be the norm is unrealistic. I have talked to so many people who struggled needlessly after someone told them that they just needed to receive an instantaneous healing from their anxiety, or depression, or bi-polar disorder, or dissociative disorder, or post-traumatic stress disorder, et.al. When healing didn't come that way, they became very upset with God for not holding up his end of the bargain. But this is a misconception about the way God operates in our world. It is not God's "fault" when things don't go the way we would like. Such thinking occurs when individuals base their theology on their experiences rather than on the Word of God.

I believe this is one of the biggest problems the 21st century church faces. Faith should shape our perceptions, our experiences, and our reactions to those things here on earth—not the other way around. The 1st century church not only survived a great deal but thrived under the adverse circumstances it faced. This is what gave us the foundations of our faith. The first Christians believed faith was a way to get to God and not a way to get things *from* God. Unlike today, their focus was on spiritual, not material, blessings.

It is sad that the church has had to refer its members with emotional and psychological problems to secular organizations to get well instead of having the means to help them within its own community. It is one of my dreams to see that situation change. If it's true that all knowledge comes from God, then the church should be enthusiastic about discovering ways to help people with these types of issues. I believe the Holy Spirit will help such an effort. Remember in the 1st century church when there were administrative and social problems in the church—and almost certainly those with emotional needs as well? The Holy Spirit instructed the disciples to choose 7 men full of the Spirit to take care of those needs while the Apostles focused on praying and teaching the Word. I believe each church needs to have its own arrangement for taking care of the needs of its people so pastors can devote themselves to the ministry of the Word and prayer.

The materials I have developed for my inpatient and outpatient treatment of emotional and psychological problems will help any church that wants to do something for its members' mental health needs. I see true faith-based therapy as also being a form of discipleship. This is why the treatment I have developed for Christians is based on both Scripture and science. Christians who follow my therapeutic model will not only be able to find emotional and psychological healing, they will also grow spiritually.

You know, the business world has recognized the need for providing employees with good, sound management skills either through in house training or by paying for outside courses. Companies do not operate on the assumption that their employees know all there is to know about managing every aspect of their departments. There are books, workshops, and seminars available that give instructions on how to manage all facets of business. I realize that the church isn't a business in the strictest sense of the word, but it is a structured organization with goals and the means to meet those goals. I think church leaders should have the same drive and motivation to offer programs that better the overall lives of their members. I know of a few churches that are already doing this, and the results are quite impressive. Their members are much healthier and are experiencing tremendous growth in many areas.

Leaders in the Christian community can't assume that people have the knowledge and skills to manage all areas of their lives. That is why I have created this book and my *Managing Your Brain Managing Your Life* DVD series to help groups as well as individuals interested in learning how to manage some of the most common problems we may face. Most serious church problems stem from members' unhealed soul wounds that lead to dysfunctional behaviors. It takes more than just repentance to resolve these types of issues. The future of the church may very well depend on whether or not believers become and stay healthy!

Additional Material by Dr. Mungadze

Dr. Jerry Mungadze has made a significant contribution to the field of psychology with his remarkable discoveries concerning the workings of the brain and the impact of emotional wounds. In this 4-part DVD series, Dr. Mungadze teaches you how to retrain your brain to resolve a host of problems involving your thinking, your emotions, and your behavior. You'll receive practical, scriptural, and scientific tools to better manage all areas of life.

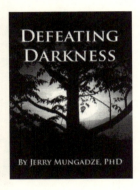

From the beginning, Satan has never been a match for God; he was defeated from the get go. In this 4-part DVD series, Dr. Mungadze explores the reality of the battle we all face in our lives and presents the truth as backed by Scripture. *Defeating Darkness* exposes the enemy and his tactics by showing you how and why the adversary is fighting for your life and how you can be spiritually equipped to fight and win by arming your brain for battle.

Would you like to know how to put the enemy and his forces in their place? This book—the first of its kind—combines the truth of Scripture with brain science to help Christians achieve victory over the enemy. You will gain a new understanding of Ephesians 6:10-18 and learn how to put on the whole armor of God in very practical ways to defeat darkness in your life and the lives of others.

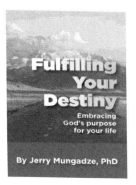

Did you know that God created you for a specific purpose? Did you know His purpose for you was predetermined before you were born? Would you like to know how to discover your personal destiny? Would you like instructions on how to overcome obstacles, avoid detours, and stay the course to fulfilling your destiny? Using clear examples from God's Word, *Fulfilling Your Destiny* provides specific, detailed insights and principles to help you discover and fulfill your own unique purpose.

To order, go to www.soundmindprograms.com. If you would like to be included on our email list to receive notice of seminars, events, and new products, you may contact us through our Sound Mind Programs website. If you are interested in therapy, you will find clinic and contact information there as well.

Made in the USA
Middletown, DE
14 September 2023

38255991R00061